Traveling in
South Carolina

Traveling in South Carolina

A Selective Guide:
Where to Go, What to Do,
What to See

by Sara Pitzer

University of South Carolina Press

Copyright © 1993 University of South Carolina

Published in Columbia, South Carolina, by the
University of South Carolina Press

Manufactured in the United States of America

Library of Congress Cataloging-in-Publication Data

Pitzer, Sara.
    Traveling in South Carolina : a selective guide : where to go,
what to do, what to see / by Sara Pitzer.
        p.   cm.
    Includes bibliographical references.
    ISBN 0–87249–868–9 (pbk. : acid free)
    1. South Carolina—Guidebooks.   I. Title.
F267.3.P58   1993
917.5704'43—dc20   93-6535

CONTENTS

Traveling in
South Carolina

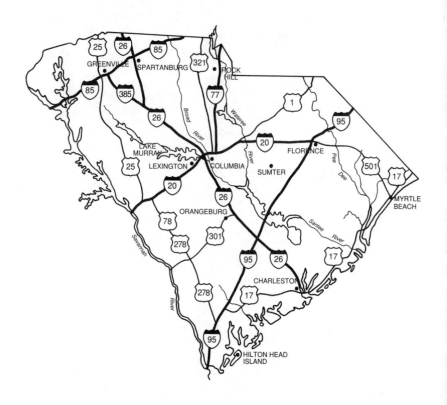

INTRODUCTION

A Few Words about Visiting South Carolina

South Carolina deserves more attention than it's had. For one thing, it is a state rich in history. It figured significantly in early colonization, the Revolutionary War, and the Civil War. South Carolinians have worked hard to preserve historic sites and to remember important people. The result is not only a lot to see but a surprising number of knowledgeable citizens with whom to discuss it.

The state also offers cultural diversity. Fine writers of fiction and poetry have lived here. South Carolinians support their artists, craftspeople, and musicians with many museums, galleries, and performance spaces.

Then you have diverse outdoor recreational possibilities, from hiking in the mountains and fishing in the Piedmont or Upcountry lakes to sunning and surfing at the beach.

All this is being discovered by growing numbers of tourists and by "transplants" whose companies are moving into the area.

One thing these people notice is that South Carolinians are almost always friendly, courteous, and helpful. People here speak when they see you walking on the street, especially in smaller towns; they wave when they pass you driving on rural roads. If you are waiting in a long line, they will chat with you to pass the time.

If you're from "up North," you may be inclined to question the sincerity of these niceties, but after you've been exposed to them for a while, the question of sincerity seems beside the point. You just enjoy the gentler ways.

But if you're accustomed to a fast pace, you'll probably

have to slow down if you want to enjoy South Carolina's people. Things simply don't happen as fast here. Once you get used to that, you'll begin to relax and have a good time.

How to Use This Book

When my daughter, Lee, was about four years old I gave her a glass of unsweetened grape juice. She sipped it and asked for sugar. I sipped from the same glass and told her it was sweet enough. She handed the glass back to me saying, "Well, it's sour on my side." I have tried to let that experience instruct me in writing this book. Rather than calling a place sweet or sour, I've tried to describe it accurately enough to let you know what it is like, but to do it without making value judgments. I don't want to say a place is wonderful and get a letter saying you thought it was awful simply because we had different ideas of what constitutes wonderfulness. Sometimes my resolve lapses. If I think I've found the world's best crabcakes in a Charleston restaurant, I just have to say so. The important thing is for you to read everything I've written with an eye to making your own judgments about whether what I've described appeals to *you*.

Also, I have written a selective guide, not an encyclopedic overview. South Carolina has lots of places that are not included here. I've concentrated on what seem like good starting places if you are just getting to know South Carolina. But the world changes. Attractions, restaurants, inns, all change their hours, their prices, even their names faster than you can put type onto paper. So that you're not disappointed or surprised, please call ahead about any place you are counting on in case something there has changed.

About South Carolina Laws

1. The legal drinking age in South Carolina is 21. Alcoholic beverages cannot be served after midnight Saturday and all day Sunday except in establishments with special permits in Charleston, Lexington, Richland counties and in most coastal

resort areas, including Hilton Head, Myrtle Beach, Charleston, and Beaufort.

2. Package store sales of alcoholic beverages are permitted between 9:00 A.M. and 7:00 P.M. Monday through Saturday.

3. It is unlawful for any person to possess an open container of beer, wine, or any other drink containing alcohol in a moving vehicle upon the highways of South Carolina.

4. Adults driving or riding in a motor vehicle in operation on public streets and highways must wear a safety belt, with the exception of occupants of public transportation vehicles, commercial vehicles, school and church buses or the like, and cars manufactured before 1966; and occupants of back seats in automobiles equipped with only lap belts in the back and not shoulder harnesses as well.

Children less than a year old riding anywhere in the vehicle must be in a child restraint seating device. Children 1–5 riding in a rear seat must use a child restraint device or a safety belt built into the vehicle. Children under 4 riding in the front seat must use a child restraint seating device. Children 4–6 riding in the front seat must be secured by a safety belt built into the vehicle.

5. Headlights must be used when windshield wipers are on.

Lowcountry
and Coastal

East Battery Street, Charleston
courtesy of Charleston Trident Visitors and Convention Bureau

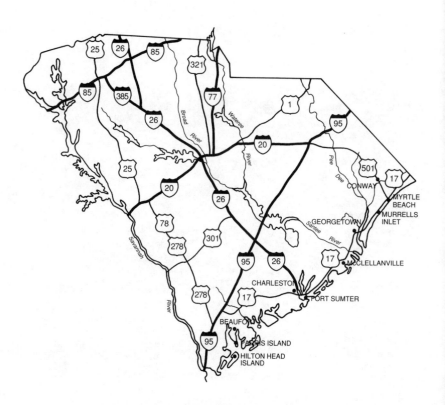

CHARLESTON

Charleston is better known than the rest of South Carolina. The city has earned a reputation for valuing its history, preserving its architecture, and sharing both with visitors with verve and hospitality.

Charleston was settled as Charles Town in 1670 by the British and in 1776 stood as a strong port against the British navy. The city was incorporated as Charleston in 1783. Rice and indigo were the area's important crops, and the wealth achieved by some planters is visible even today in the historic plantations.

Not only did the hardships of the Civil War ruin an economy that was already slowing; numerous sites around the city also reflect the ravages of fighting and the related problems of slavery.

You can't see all there is to see in Charleston in a weekend or even in a week. You can't even come close. The keys to an enjoyable visit here are planning your time and wearing comfortable shoes. This is not a city where you can comfortably drive from one site to the next, unless you're willing to settle for what you can see from the car. The streets are narrow and busy; parking is a problem. The best way to manage your sightseeing is to plan on visiting a number of sites within walking distance of one another and find a central place to park nearby.

You'll quickly notice that Charleston is a city of walkers and a city of talkers. Mostly the walkers are tourists, and the talkers are local residents stopping to give directions and maybe a little history lesson at the same time. It's a recurring scene: two or three people standing on a corner, at least one of them holding a map, and another person standing by, talking and pointing. This is a nice thing about Charleston. Most of the time you don't even have to ask for help; people who see that you're confused simply offer it.

Walking in the historic district will give you the best view of some of Charleston's most famous features: the Battery, Rainbow Row, the Old Slave Mart, and the market.

The Battery, at the waterfront where the Ashley and Cooper rivers meet, consists of White Point Park and the nearby residential area. The name comes from the heavy fortification that defended the city against attack by sea in earlier times. Around the park, cannon stand to represent wars in which the city was involved, and monuments commemorate Charleston's important people and historic moments.

Rainbow Row, running from 79 to 107 East Bay Street, gets its name from the pastel colors of its houses. In the mid- and late 1700s the buildings were waterfront stores with living quarters on the second story. By the early 1900s they had become slums. Recent restoration has turned them into picturesque, highly valuable real estate.

The Old Slave Mart, at 6 Chalmers Street, was one of the markets at which slaves were sold after 1856, when the city forbade selling them in the open streets. The Gothic Revival building included a jail to confine the slaves and a large yard. In recent years, as the Old Slave Mart Museum, the building served as a museum of African American art and history. At present it is closed.

Charleston's market is sometimes confused with the Old Slave Mart. In the 19th century, not slaves but produce, fish, and meat were sold there. Today the open-air market, between Church Street and East Bay Street, rents stalls under roof in long pavilions to local crafts people and retailers. Their offerings range from clothing and jewelry to lithograph reproductions of pressed-flower pictures to dried-bean mixes for many-bean soups to imported odds and ends. Between Church Street and Meeting Street all kinds of pricey, trendy specialty shops come and go. The entire market area attracts tourists all year. Wandering through the stalls and shops can take hours and be a lot of fun. You probably won't get away without succumbing to the temptation to buy something. But in addition to the carnival atmosphere here, Charleston offers a mind-boggling array of

historic sites and important architectural structures. Some visitors say studying the architecture in Charleston is better than going to Boston because the buildings are just as old, the quality
just as fine, and it's all more accessible. With the multitude of
possibilities for seeing historic homes, government buildings,
forts, plantations, and gardens, you can be paralyzed just trying
to figure out where to start.

The following suggestions, intended to help reduce your
confusion, do not cover every possible place to visit in
Charleston, but they do represent the major and most frequently visited attractions.

Activities and Attractions

CHARLESTON VISITORS RECEPTION AND TRANSPORTATION CENTER
    375 Meeting Street
    (803) 853–8000
    Open daily 8:30 A.M. to 5:30 P.M. Closes one-half hour
    earlier in November, December, February. Closed
    Thanksgiving, Christmas, New Year's Day.

No matter what you want to see and do in Charleston, your
first stop should be the Visitors Center, one of the best run in
the country.

A sign in the window says "Welcome to Charleston" in nine
different languages. A plaque outside explains that the center
is in the restored Railroad Freight Depot, built in 1856.

The depot works beautifully as a central information site
for visitors. The wide building is light, and its high ceilings
keep you from feeling crowded even when the place is busy. As
you come through the entry, you stop to study a model of the
peninsula, showing the Ashley and Cooper rivers, the buildings of the city, and its streets. Then a nine-screen display with
changing pictures, music, and narration gives you a "media
event" impression of Charleston.

On the walls, old and new maps in large scale help you see
how the city has changed. At video stations marked "How to
Visit Charleston" you can call up information on user-

activated screens and request additional advice on the telephones. It's not uncommon to see tourists with maps in hand
noting directions from their telephone conversations.

Displays of old silver and pottery, sweetgrass baskets, and
area artifacts add interest.

At the service desk you can get information about special
events, ask general questions, and buy various books and
booklets about Charleston. Free brochures are available in
displays along both sides of the hall.

At the far end of the building, at a small souvenir counter,
you can buy tickets for the twenty-minute film "Forever
Charleston," which is shown every half hour. They call it a
"spectacular," and, indeed, it is more than a film. It is a combination of slides shown on twenty-seven computerized pro-
jectors, coordinated with recorded music, city sound, and
narration by Charleston people. The staff at the Visitors Center show obvious pride in presenting it.

Another feature of the center, one that doesn't get anything
like the publicity it deserves, is its spacious, clean restrooms,
comfortably accessible to the handicapped. When you're looking for a restroom, nothing else matters much.

Next to the Visitors Center building you'll find the transportation depot, where you can pick up one of the shuttles for
the Downtown Area Shuttle (DASH), which come along every
fifteen minutes and make loops through the areas of major interest and back to the terminal. Individual tickets are 50 cents
and day-long passes are only $1.00. An intelligent way to use
this service is to take a few rides as you figure out which areas
you'd like to walk through to see things more closely. You'll be
able to pick up maps at the center showing the various routes.

Another service housed in the center is SCAT, where you can
buy tour, concert, and theater tickets at one central location.

PRESERVATION SOCIETY OF CHARLESTON
    147 King Street
    (803) 723–4381
    Open Monday through Saturday 10:00 A.M. to 5:00 P.M.

Here you'll find an excellent bookstore featuring practically every book in print about Charleston and South Carolina, ranging from history to cooking. You'll find an assortment of local crafts and gift items including the sweetgrass baskets of an exceptionally talented basketmaker, Henrietta Snype.

The Preservation Society also sponsors the annual Fall Candlelight Tours, which run from the end of September to the end of October. Call for specifics.

GIBBES MUSEUM OF ART
     135 Meeting Street
     (803) 722–2706
     Open Tuesday through Saturday 10:00 A.M. to 5:00 P.M.,
     Sunday and Monday 1:00 P.M. to 5:00 P.M.
     Admission $3.00 for adults, $2.00 for students and senior
     citizens, $1.00 for children to age 12.

The museum houses one of the better collections of fine arts in the Southeast, with exhibits of portraits and other paintings, sculpture, Japanese wood-block prints, and art objects. A unique specialty of the museum is the collection of 450 18th- and 19th-century American miniatures, including a sizable number by Charles Fraser and others by Henry Benbridge and John Ramadge. You can call ahead to arrange a viewing of a twenty-minute film about the miniatures. The museum also has an important collection of about 500 18th- and 19th-century American portraits. As one visitor said, "This is a great museum to visit with your kids because it has a smattering of everything, and about the time they get bored with one thing you're on to something else." In the uncommonly nice gift shop you'll find books, note cards, and the other art-related items.

CHARLESTON MUSEUM
     360 Meeting Street
     (803) 722–2996
     Open Monday through Saturday 9:00 A.M. to 5:00 P.M.,
     Sunday 1:00 P.M. to 5:00 P.M. Closed holidays.

Admission to the museum $5.00 for adults, $3.00 for
children 3–17, free for children under 3.
Admission to the museum, the Aiken-Rhett House, the
Heyward-Washington House, and the Joseph Manigault
House $15.00 for adults, $9.00 for children 3–17, free for
children under 3.
Visitors may purchase a one-site or all-site ticket at the
museum or at any of the houses listed above.

This is the oldest museum in the country. It was opened
in 1773. It owns the houses listed above and features displays
on history, natural history, archaeology, ornithology, and
decorative arts. It also has children's exhibits to touch, with
emphasis on Lowcountry influences. A silver collection
contains English and Charleston pieces dating back to the
1700s.

AIKEN-RHETT HOUSE

48 Elizabeth Street
(803) 723–1159
Admission to the Aiken-Rhett House $5.00 for adults,
$3.00 for children 3–17, free for children under 3.
Admission to the Aiken-Rhett House, the Heyward-
Washington House, the Joseph Manigault House, and
the Charleston Museum $15.00 for adults, $9.00 for
children 3–17, free for children under 3.
Visitors may purchase a one-site or all-site ticket at the
Aiken-Rhett House or any of the other locations listed
above.

This house is one of those owned by the Charleston Museum. It was built in the early 1800s by a wealthy merchant
and remodeled by Gov. William Aiken, who lived in it until
the late 1800s. During the Civil War, General Beauregard used
it as his headquarters. The rooms are furnished in the popular
Charlestonian styles of the period. When you tour this building, it is important to understand that it is a preservation
rather than a restoration.

HEYWARD-WASHINGTON HOUSE

87 Church Street

(803) 722–0354

Admission to the Heyward-Washington House $5.00 for adults, $3.00 for children 3–17, free for children under 3. Admission to the Heyward-Washington House, the Aiken-Rhett House, the Joseph Manigault House, and the Charleston

Museum $15.00 for adults, $9.00 for children 3–17, free for children under 3.

Visitors may purchase a one-site or all-site ticket at the Heyward-Washington House or any of the other three locations listed above.

Thomas Heyward, Jr., one of the signers of the Declaration of Independence, lived in this house, which was built in 1772. Today it is notable especially for its fine collection of 18th-century Charleston-made furniture. You'll also find here the only Charleston kitchen house (behind the main house) that is open for public tour. The kitchen house has a beehive oven and an assortment of old utensils used for cooking and cleaning.

JOSEPH MANIGAULT HOUSE

350 Meeting Street

(803) 723–2926

Admission to the Joseph Manigault House $5.00 for adults, $3.00 for children 3–17, free for children under 3.

Admission to the Joseph Manigault House, the Aiken-Rhett House, the Heyward-Washington House, and the Charleston Museum $15.00 for adults, $9.00 for children 3–17, free for children under 3.

Visitors may purchase a one-site or all-site ticket at the Joseph Manigault House or any of the other three locations listed above.

Joseph Manigault had a lot of money and a brother, Gabriel, who was an architect. Gabriel designed this expensive Federal-style house for Joseph. It was built in 1803. The interior architectural details have remained intact over the years with very little alteration. An unsupported circular stairway provides a dramatic focal point.

You get a flash of insight into the way Manigault lived when you discover that public rooms such as the dining room are lavishly decorated while such private rooms as bedrooms are simple.

The interior reflects an interesting attitude toward wood materials. Doors on the first floor are made of cypress grained to look like mahogany; on the second floor they are grained to look like satinwood.

Here you will see the first indoor powder room built in the city. And the place is special also because it is one of the few where a gate house remains standing on the property.

As glorious as it is, the house almost didn't make it through hard times. In 1920 it was a broken-down boarding house in danger of being demolished. For a while a service station operated where the garden is. A number of Charleston people and businesses, as well as some people who wintered in the area, got involved in its restoration. Eventually even the dean of the Harvard School of Architecture got involved. When you tour here you see the results of their cooperative efforts and those of people who donated to the house/museum everything from Waterford glass to Louis XV furniture. The human story seems every bit as valuable as the architecture and furnishings.

NATHANIEL RUSSELL HOUSE
    51 Meeting Street
    (803) 722–3405
    Open Monday through Saturday 10:00 A.M. to 5:00 P.M.,
    Sunday 2:00 P.M. to 5:00 P.M.
    Admission $5.00 for adults and for children 6 and over,
    free for children under 6. Admission for both the
    Nathaniel Russell House and the Edmonston-Alston
    House $8.00 for adults and for children 6 and over, free
    for children under 6.

The first thing you notice here is the great "flying" staircase curving up three stories with no apparent support. Built in 1808 by a wealthy merchant from Rhode Island, the house is considered one of the best examples of the Adam style in the country. It is made of two kinds of brick and surrounded by a large garden. Inside, the oval drawing rooms are another unusual feature. Many of the period furnishings were made by Charleston craftsmen. The house is also noted for its beautifully detailed and crafted wood and plaster work.

EDMONSTON-ALSTON HOUSE

21 East Battery
(803) 722–7171
Open Tuesday through Saturday 10:00 A.M. to 5:00 P.M., Sunday and Monday 1:30 P.M. to 5:00 P.M. Last tour begins at 4:30 P.M.
Admission $5.00 for adults and for children 6 and over, free for children under 6. Admission for both the Edmonston-Alston House and the Nathaniel Russell House $8.00 for adults and for children 6 and over, free for children under 6.

This house is a good example of what a lot of well-to-do Charleston people liked in the early 19th century. Charles Edmonston, a wealthy merchant from Scotland who was better at making money than at keeping it, built it in the late 1820s. In 1839 the house was sold to pay off his debts. The new owner, Charles Alston, had it done over in Greek Revival style. Visitors particularly enjoy the view overlooking the harbor and appreciate finding the home still furnished with the Alston family belongings. Most of them are pieces from the mid-19th century, more of them American than English. A pair of Cornelius and Co. chandeliers, made in 1835 and purchased in Philadelphia, must have excited comment when they were installed in the house, much as they attract oohs and ahs today.

CALHOUN MANSION

16 Meeting Street
(803) 722–8205
Open Wednesday through Sunday 10:00 A.M. to 4:00 P.M. Closed Monday and Tuesday.

Admission $10.00 for adults, $5.00 for children 6–15, free for children under 6.

A Victorian showplace from the time it was built in 1876, the Calhoun Mansion overwhelms you with its size. It has 24,000 square feet (these days a house with 3,000 square feet is considered very large) divided into twenty-five rooms. The elaborate plaster moldings, woodworking, and tile floors vary from room to room, and a skylight in the forty-five-foot-high ceiling illuminates the ballroom.

Dock Street Theatre
135 Church Street
(803) 720–3968
Open Monday through Friday 8:30 A.M. to 4:00 P.M. unless play rehearsals or preparations are under way.
Admission free except for performances.

One of America's first playhouses, built in 1735, stood here, but the building you see here now combines a reconstruction of that early Georgian theater and the restoration of the Planter's Hotel, which stood on the same site and was a favorite haunt of the well-to-do in the 1800s. The hotel deteriorated after the Civil War and wasn't restored until 1935, when the city of Charleston took on the job as a WPA project. Some of the material used inside came from old Charleston houses.

Old Exchange and Provost Dungeon
Corner of East Bay Street and Broad Street
(803) 727–2165
Open Monday through Sunday 9:00 A.M. to 5:00 P.M.
Closed holidays.
Admission $3.00 for adults, $1.50 for children 6–12, free for children under 6. Discount for senior citizens.

This building (c. 1767–1771) is notable because so much of historic importance happened here over such a long period of time. The Old Exchange was first a customs house. The British kept political prisoners in the dungeon during the Revolution. South Carolina's signers of the Declaration of Independence were elected, the U.S. Constitution was ratified, a Charleston rebel was hanged by the British, and George Washington partied—all in this building. In 1818 it was the Federal Post Office. Today it is managed by the city and is open for tours and available for social events.

Historic Churches

Charleston got the nickname "The Holy City" because so many churches flourished here. In the beginning that was probably because South Carolina had the broadest laws to guarantee religious freedom of any of the thirteen colonies. Today Charleston has 136 established churches, though not all in historic buildings, of course. The most comprehensive listing of churches is the one appearing every Saturday in the *Charleston News and Courier*, giving addresses, service times, and in some cases telephone numbers. The simplest way to see the interior of a church is to attend a service, but many of the historically and architecturally important churches invite visitors at other times as well. Circumstances and touring hours change, so it is a good idea to telephone in advance any church you wish to tour. The following list is not exhaustive but covers the most frequently recognized churches in Charleston.

BETH ELOHIM
> 90 Hasell Street
> (803) 723–1090
> Open Monday through Friday 10:00 A.M. to noon.
> Donations appreciated.

This 1840 structure houses a synagogue that is considered the originating place of Reform Judaism in the United States. The building, which replaces one destroyed by fire in 1838, is considered one of the best examples of Greek Revival architecture in the country.

BRITH SHOLOM BETH ISRAEL CONGREGATION
182 Rutledge Avenue
(803) 577–6599
Not open for public tours.

By Charleston standards this building is relatively new, built in 1945. Its congregation, however, dates back to the 1850s. The original synagogue, dedicated in 1856, stood at the corner of St. Philip and Calhoun Streets. In 1945 a new structure was built on Rutledge Avenue, incorporating many elements from the beautiful interior of the St. Philip's Street sanctuary. Because you cannot tour the synagogue, you might wish to attend services.

CIRCULAR CONGREGATIONAL CHURCH
150 Meeting Street
(803) 577–6400

This church is notable for having established the first Sunday School in South Carolina. The building is the fourth to occupy the site as a church and includes some brick from the building that burned during the earthquake of 1886. Like its predecessors on the site, this church really is round. Although it began in 1681 as the Independent Church of Charles Town, the Circular Congregational Church today is affiliated with the United Church of Christ, and the Presbyterian Church in the U.S., and the United Presbyterian Church of the U.S.A.

The church makes no formal arrangements on a scheduled basis for accommodating sightseers, but when the doors are open you are welcome to come in, providing you respect the sanctuary and avoid tracking in heavy dirt.

EMANUEL AFRICAN METHODIST EPISCOPAL CHURCH
110 Calhoun Street
(803) 722–2561
Visits may be arranged by calling the number above.

This was one of the country's first African American congregations. It was organized in its own building in 1818 but was later closed by authorities to avoid insurrection. The congregation reorganized in 1865 but didn't build the new building until 1891. Many important black leaders have been associated with the congregation.

FRENCH HUGUENOT CHURCH
Corner of Church Street and Queen Street
(803) 722–4385
To arrange guided visits call Wednesdays from
10:00 A.M. to noon or Monday, Thursday, Friday
9:00 A.M. to 1:00 P.M.

The only independent Huguenot Church in America, this has been a place of worship for French Huguenots since 1687. The existing building is the fourth on the site, built in 1845. The Huguenot Liturgy of 1737 of Neuchâtel and Vallangin, which was conducted in French for about a century and a half, is now recited in English at 10:30 services on Sunday mornings.

ST. MARY'S CATHOLIC CHURCH
89 Hasell Street
(803) 722–7696

The congregation was established in 1789, making St. Mary's the oldest Roman Catholic Church in South Carolina. The existing structure was built in 1839 to replace the building that burned a year earlier. Of particular interest at St. Mary's are the stained-glass windows and oil paintings in the interior and the graveyard, among the most international in the city.

ST. MATTHEW'S LUTHERAN CHURCH
405 King Street
(803) 723–1611
Open for visitors Monday, Wednesday, Thursday, and
Friday from 8:30 A.M. to 4:30 P.M., Saturday from
9:00 A.M. to noon. Closed Sunday afternoon.

Visually, the outstanding features here are the stained-glass windows depicting biblical scenes and the 297-foot steeple built in 1872. The building burned in 1965 and was rebuilt. This church is considered one of Charleston's most beautiful. Literature offering more information about St. Matthew's is available at the church.

St. Michael's Episcopal Church
80 Meeting Street (Meeting at Broad Street)
(803) 723–0603

St. Michael's is the oldest church building in Charleston. It was built between 1751 and 1762. The architecture is Georgian style. Inside, the original pulpit and wooden box pews are still in use. George Washington worshiped here. Time and hurricanes have weakened the building and eroded its surfaces, but the church membership works aggressively to preserve it as a historic landmark.

St. Philip's Episcopal Church
146 Church Street
(803) 722–7734
Open for visitors Monday through Friday 11 A.M. to 4:00 P.M.

St. Philip's, founded in 1670, is the mother church of the Episcopal Diocese of South Carolina. Earlier buildings burned, and the present building was finished in 1838. The church cemetery contains the graves of important personages from earlier years, including Edward Rutledge, signer of the Declaration of Independence and state governor; Charles Pinckney, a signer of the United States Constitution and state governor; and John C. Calhoun, U.S. senator, secretary of war, vice-president, and secretary of state, successively.

Nearby Gardens and Nature Preserves

CHARLES TOWNE LANDING NATURE PRESERVE AND HISTORIC SITE
1500 Old Towne Road
(Across the Ashley River just northwest of the city, on SC
171 between I–26 and US 17)
(803) 556–4450
Open daily 9:00 A.M. to 5:00 P.M., except open to 6:00 P.M.
Memorial Day through Labor Day. Closed December 24
and 25.
Admission $5 for adults, $2.50 for senior citizens, $2.50 for
children 6–14, and free for children under 6.

Visiting Charles Towne Landing, you get a glimpse of daily
life as it would have been in Charleston, South Carolina's first
permanent English settlement, during the colony's early years,
beginning in 1670. You can board the full-scale replica of the
17th-century trading vessel *Adventure* and roam through replica colonial buildings in the Settlers' Life Area. In the 1670
Experimental Crop Garden you'll see in season the kinds of
vegetables and cash crops the settlers grew. In the natural habitat zoo you'll see the animals that would have wandered the
area and probably, sometimes, threatened the garden.

Equally fascinating, the original boundaries of the colony have
been uncovered, and you can see the site of the original fortified
town that archeologists will be exploring in the future.

History aside, Charles Towne Landing refreshes you with
the beauty of its landscaping and flowering shrubs and its
walking and biking paths. You can rent bikes. If exercise is the
last thing you want, try a narrated tram tour for just a dollar.

CYPRESS GARDENS
15 miles north of Charleston off US 52
Open daily 9:00 A.M. to 5:00 P.M.
Admission mid-February through April $6 for adults, $5 for
senior citizens, $2 for children 6–16; May through January
adults and senior citizens a dollar less.
(803) 553–0515

This park, owned by the City of Charleston Department of Parks, is a good place for walking or boating to enjoy the color of cultivated flowering plants such as camellias in winter and wisteria and azaleas in spring. Indigenous ferns and foliage flourish, providing cover for all kinds of wildlife including alligators, turtles, and birds, Magnificant old cypress trees growing in a freshwater lake set off the gardens.

Nearby Plantations

If you think of plantations as once having been huge, self-sufficient homestead/farms, you get the basic idea. The crops usually were cotton, indigo, and rice as well as livestock and produce for food. The homestead included not only extended families but also the vast numbers of slaves used to work the crops, maintain the property, and serve the owners. Although men were considered plantation masters, women, usually wives, often bore the responsibility of managing the plantation. In such cases, women oversaw not just the house and slaves but also the gardens, livestock operation, and crops, while the men handled business transactions.

Today the plantations in the Charleston area differ in the nature of their preservation and restoration and in the attractions they offer tourists. You can piece together an interesting picture of old plantation life by visiting several different places.

BOONE HALL PLANTATION
8 miles north of Charleston on US 17
(803) 884-4371
Open April 1 to Labor Day 8:30 A.M. to 6:30 P.M. Monday through Saturday, 1:00 P.M. to 5:00 P.M. Sunday; Labor Day to March 31 9:00 A.M. to 5:00 P.M. Monday through Saturday, 1:00 P.M. to 4:00 P.M. Sunday. Closed Thanksgiving and Christmas.
Admission $7.50 for adults, $5.00 for senior citizens, $3.00 for children 6–12, and free for children under 6.

You enter the plantation through a long drive of eighty-eight old live oaks swathed in Spanish moss, famous as the model for the approach to Tara in *Gone with the Wind*. Nearly a hundred of the trees were planted in the mid-1700s, and it is remarkable that so many have survived. Boone Hall was a cotton plantation of 17,000 acres. Today visitors may tour the first floor of the renovated Greek Revival-style mansion and walk in the formal camellia and azalea gardens. Also on the property are nine original slave cabins built from brick made on the property, and a gin house (for cotton, not booze!).

DRAYTON HALL

> 9 miles northwest of Charleston on SC 61
> (803) 766–0188
> Open daily November through February 10:00 A.M. to 3:00 P.M.; March through October 10:00 A.M. to 4:00 P.M. Guided tours begin on the hour. Closed Thanksgiving, Christmas, and New Year's Day.
> Admission $6.00 for adults, $3.00 for students (including college students with a valid ID), free for children under 6.

Be sure to visit here if you have a special interest in preserved (rather than restored) architecture and in fine interior finishing.

Drayton Hall, built between 1738 and 1742 on a rise overlooking the Ashley River, stands as an outstanding example of Georgian-Palladian architecture, remarkable in that it remains in virtually its original state. (The building belongs to the National Trust for Historic Preservation.) The interior has richly detailed, hand-crafted ornamentation including a sculpted plaster ceiling and elaborate woodworking. Some of the original paint remains on the walls.

The rooms are not furnished. This offers the visitor a rare chance to concentrate on the architecture and craftsmanship alone. It also creates fabulous acoustics. If you are visiting around Christmas, it would be worth inquiring about the concerts of West African work songs, during which, as one staff member put it, "the music just seems to roll through the doors."

MAGNOLIA PLANTATION AND GARDENS
10 miles northwest of Charleston on SC 61
(803) 571–1266
Open daily 8:00 A.M. to 5:00 P.M. If you are on the grounds
by 5:00 P.M., you may stay until dusk.
Admission to the historic gardens and grounds June
through February $8.00 for adults, $6.00 for teenagers,
$4.00 for children 4–12; March through May all $1.00
higher. Plantation house tour $4.00 additional for each
person. Swamp garden $4.00 additional for adults, $3.00
additional for children and teens. To visit only the swamp
garden, $6.00 for adults, $3.00 for children and teens.

Garden writers have called Magnolia Gardens, America's
oldest gardens, the most beautiful in the South. Even if you
don't want to get into the garden-rating wars, you'll find the
bloom on these fifty acres of formal and informal gardens
awesome. The display includes 900 varieties of camellias and
250 of azaleas, as well as other flowering shrubs, bulbs, and
bedding plants. Gardeners plant more than 150,000 new
bulbs every year.

The plantation has been in the family of Drayton descen-
dants since the late 1600s. The Draytons made their gardens a
priority from the beginning. The plantation's current owner,
Drayton Hastie, tries to introduce as many new plants to the
property as possible. The result is color and bloom almost
year-round in formal gardens, theme gardens, and cottage-
style gardens. It takes a staff of eighteen gardeners to maintain
Magnolia Gardens.

Also on the property, Audubon Swamp Garden, sixty acres
of cypress and tupelo swamp that you get to on small foot-
bridges and boardwalks, gives visitors an up-close look at all
kinds of swamp wildlife in an essentially unspoiled setting.

Children enjoy the petting zoo. Hiking and biking trails, an
observation tower, and picnic areas give you opportunities to
see the broader landscape and rest a while over lunch.

You may also tour the plantation house. The Hastie family
lived in it until 1976. Though now you find a gift shop on the
ground floor, the second story remains much the same as it was

shortly after the Civil War, giving you an idea of the near-spartan nature of life during Reconstruction. The top floor, which used to be bedrooms, is a gallery for the works of area artists.

MIDDLETON PLACE
> 14 miles northwest of Charleston on SC 61.
> (803) 556–6020
> Open daily 9:00 A.M. to 5:00 P.M.
> Admission to grounds and stableyard June through February $9.00 for adults, $4.50 for children 6–12, free for children under 6; March through May $10.00 for adults, $5.00 for children 6–12, free for children under 6. Admission to house and museum $5.00 additional year-round.

This plantation claims America's oldest formal landscaped gardens. They were laid out in 1741 along the banks of the Ashley River as part of the estate according to a plan probably inspired by 18th-century French design. The original garden took more than a decade to finish. When informal, naturalistic plantings came into vogue this plantation's managers added them without destroying any of the original formal gardens.

The Civil War, the earthquake of 1886, and financially hard years in between diminished the property's early splendor. Sherman's troops burned the house that had been built in 1755. The family eventually restored part of the building as their home. Today the Middleton Place Foundation (a non-profit organization) operates the home as a museum. Guides lead tours through rooms furnished in plantation style.

Nearby Military Sites

PATRIOTS POINT NAVAL AND MARITIME MUSEUM
> Charleston Harbor
> 40 Patriots Point Road
> Mt. Pleasant
> (803) 884–2727
> Open daily April 1 through September 30 9:00 A.M. to 7:30

P.M.; October 1 through March 31 9:00 A.M. to 6:30 P.M.
Closed Christmas.
Admission $8 for adults, $4.50 for children 5–12, free for
children under 5.

A mile from the Cooper River Bridge you find the world's
largest naval and maritime museum with four permanently
moored ships, twenty aircraft, and the World War II aircraft
carrier *Yorktown*. You can tour the *Yorktown*, the destroyer
Laffey, the Coast Guard cutter *Ingham*, the submarine *Cla-
magore*, and the nuclear-power ship *Savannah*.

The *Yorktown* is the centerpiece of the museum. Commissioned April 15, 1943, the carrier served in combat at Truk,
the Marianas, Iwo Jima, and Okinawa. On a more peaceful
mission in 1968, the *Yorktown* picked up the crew of *Apollo
8*, the first manned spacecraft to circle the moon.

On the *Yorktown* you'll see the flight and hangar decks and
the ship's sickbay, bridge, and ready room. Aircraft from
World War II through Vietnam are on display. The film "The
Fighting Lady" shows the story of the ship's years of service.

Also on board, a snack bar, cafeteria, and gift shop remind
you that this former war ship is now a tourist attraction.

FORT SUMTER
Accessible only through Fort Sumter Tours
Charleston City Marina
17 Lockwood Blvd
(803) 722–1691
Tours run daily March through November from the
Charleston City Marina at 9:30 A.M., noon, and 2:30 P.M.
From Patriots Point (see p. 27) tours leave at 10:45 A.M.,
1:30 P.M., and 4:00 P.M. In December, January, and
February tours leave daily from Charleston City Marina
at 2:30 P.M. and from Patriots Point daily at 1:30 P.M.
Admission $8.50 for adults, $4.25 for children under 12,
free for children under 6.

Fort Sumter, situated on a man-made island, took thirty-one
years to build; construction ended the day after Christmas in

1860. The fort was initially occupied by Union soldiers who had been at Fort Moultrie. The first shot of the Civil War was fired by Confederate troops attacking the fort. After thirty-four hours, the Yankee troops surrendered and Confederates took over. Fort Sumter remains important to some Southerners as a historic symbol of resistance. When the Rebels left in 1865, nothing much remained but rubble. Today a museum and gift shop serve all who visit, from North or South.

The tour to Fort Sumter, for which details are given above, comprises an hour and fifteen minutes in the harbor on a sightseeing yacht and an hour in Fort Sumter. It is narrated by National Park Service historians.

FORT MOULTRIE

West Middle Street on Sullivan's Island
10 miles east of Charleston off SC 703
(803) 883–3123
Open daily 6 A.M. to 5:00 P.M., except open until 6:00 P.M. from Memorial Day through Labor Day. Closed Christmas Day. Admission free.

Across the channel from Fort Sumter, Fort Moultrie is part of the Fort Sumter National Monument. Fort Moultrie began as a log structure built in 1776. From it, a troop of South Carolinians moved against the British fleet on June 28, 1776, to score the first American victory in the American Revolution. The fort was rebuilt in 1809 on the same site. Present restoration shows how America's coastline defense has evolved over the past 200 years. You can explore the fort yourself or take one of the tours. The tour schedule varies, so you'll need to call ahead.

Lodging

Your lodging choices in Charleston include a full measure of standard hotel and motel chains plus an interesting assortment of historic hotels and bed and breakfast inns, as well as bed and breakfast *homes*, where homeowners provide a room and breakfast in their private residences. Each possibility has its advantages. The chain motels tend to cost a little less than historic hotels and inns. Inns offer highly individualistic accommodations and a nice opportunity to meet other travelers. Bed and breakfast homes often give you a chance to get to know a Charleston family personally but do not charge the low price of European tradition. In Charleston, rooms in bed and breakfast homes cost more than other rooms.

The following listings give a general range of rates for each hostelry because rates not only change often but also vary with the season. Although they tend to be high during peak seasons, such as early spring, you can often enjoy discounts at other times of the year. Accommodations in the historic district and on the peninsula cost more than comparable quarters in outlying areas. Rates are highest in spring and fall, lowest in summer and winter. Wherever you stay, you may qualify for discounts, but you usually have to ask to get them.

Bed and Breakfast Homes

CHARLESTON SOCIETY BED AND BREAKFAST
    Eleanor Rogers, Coordinator
    84 Murray Boulevard
    Charleston, SC 29401
    (803) 723–4948
    Rates: $72–$200

The best way to arrange bed and breakfast home stays is through this reservation service, which matches guests and participating private homes offering bed and breakfast according to the tastes and preferences of the guests and the hosts, trying to match both personal interests and individual habits such as smoking. You have to answer a short questionnaire as part of making your reservation.

All the homes are historic properties within walking distance of restaurants, all have private baths, and all provide continental breakfast. Some have private entrances to guest rooms.

Write for a brochure or call from 9:00 A.M. to 6:00 P.M. Monday through Friday for reservations.

Historic Hotels and Inns

ANCHORAGE
>   26 Vendue Range
>   Charleston, SC 29401
>   (800) 421–2952 or (803) 723–8300
>   Rates: $80 to $180 for rooms, to $220 for suites

Liz Tucker owns the inn. Her daughter, Elizabeth, serves as the innkeeper. Liz declares herself an Anglophile. Her passion provides the theme for this new inn in an old building by the harbor. She furnished the renovated antebellum warehouse with pieces chosen to reflect the English heritage and maritime activities of South Carolina. A furniture maker in High Point, North Carolina, designed and built the elegant reproductions of 17th-century English pieces especially for the Anchorage. Tea is served every afternoon by the fireplace in the English library.

Rates include a full breakfast in the dining room or continental breakfast in your room.

The inn has nineteen rooms, all with private bath, television, and telephones. Two of the rooms are luxury suites with Jacuzzi tubs.

ANSONBOROUGH INN
>   21 Hasell Street
>   Charleston, SC 29401
>   (800) 522–2073 or (803) 723–1655
>   Rates: $79 to $150

The original plan in renovating this three-story warehouse in the historic district was to turn it into condos, so each unit has a kitchen and roomy sitting area in addition to bedrooms. It's nice for longer stays and downright luxurious for shorter visits.

The center of the second and third floors was opened to the ceiling, where skylights let in natural light that shines strikingly through massive beams into the lobby. Old heart pine beams and locally fired red brick form some part of every suite. The ceilings are all at least twenty feet high. The place gives the visitor a sense of great spaciousness and peace. Continental breakfast is served each morning in the lobby, wine and cheese in the afternoon. If you want some simple cookware for your kitchen, all you have to do is ask. For that matter, if you want breakfast delivered to your room, asking will bring that too. The staff here are particularly friendly and eager to please.

The inn has thirty-seven suites, all with telephones and television.

BARKSDALE HOUSE INN
   27 George Street
   Charleston, SC 29401
   (803) 577–4800
   Rates: $79 to $150

Originally a 1778 town house, this renovated building now offers guest rooms, each featuring a different motif, ranging from French to Oriental. The inn is furnished with a mix of antiques and period reproductions, and flowers everywhere brighten the rooms.

Rates include breakfast on a silver tray and as much help as you need in arranging tours and making reservations for dinner or the theater.

The inn has ten rooms, all with private bath, television, and telephone, five with whirlpool, six with fireplace.

BELVEDERE
   40 Rutledge Avenue
   Charleston, SC 29401
   (803) 722–0973
   Rate: $95

Belvedere is one of the smaller inns in Charleston and one of the more interesting. Its interior is older than its exterior. The actual building is a Colonial Revival-style white mansion, built about 1900. The woodwork inside was salvaged from an 18th-century home at Belvedere Plantation nearby in the 1920s when that property was leveled to build a golf course. Each guest room here has an ornamental fireplace and fine antique furniture. Guests have the opportunity to mingle during breakfast, served in the upstairs central hall looking out over the Ashley River and Colonial Lake, or over evening sherry in the formal dining room downstairs.

Rates include continental breakfast.

The inn has three rooms, all with private bath and television.

Two Meeting Street

> 2 Meeting Street
> Charleston, SC 29401
> (803) 723–7322
> Rates: $90 to $130

This renovated 1892 Queen Anne mansion is one of Charleston's best known inns. It is filled with family antiques. Tiffany stained-glass windows and carved-oak paneling draw your attention as soon as you enter the house. From the piazzas you can see the Battery park. Sipping afternoon sherry on the piazza watching people in the park is a favorite guest activity. The guest rooms are luxuriously furnished with period furniture. On the third floor you'll find everything in tip-top shape because Hurricane Hugo blew away part of the roof and the Spells had to renovate the flooded third floor completely.

Rates include continental breakfast. The inn has nine rooms, all with private bath. Television on request.

John Rutledge House Inn

> 116 Broad Street
> Charleston, SC 29401
> (800) 476–9741 or (803) 723–7999
> Rates: $105 to $185 for rooms, $200 to $250 for suites

John Rutledge, one of the signers of the U.S. Constitution, lived here. The house was built in 1763. Its original plaster moldings, marble mantles, and parquet floors have been returned to their early glory, making it easy to imagine the parties attended by people responsible for much of our nation's early history. The guest rooms are furnished with antiques and period reproductions.

Rates include continental breakfast.

The inn has nineteen rooms in the main house and two carriage houses, all with private bath, television and telephone, some with Jacuzzis, some with wheelchair access.

KINGS COURTYARD INN

198 King Street
Charleston, SC 29401
(800) 845–6119 or (803) 723–7000
Rates: $85 to $150 for rooms, suites $150 to $190

This is a well established, well run inn housed in a three-story 1853 Greek Revival-style building. Plant-filled courtyards offer quiet refuge from the streets and make a pleasant place for coffee or cocktails. Guest rooms contain period reproduction furnishings.

Continental breakfast is included in the rates.

The inn has thirty-four rooms, all with private bath, television, and telephone; some with fireplace, some with wheelchair access.

MAISON DUPRE

East Bay at George Street
Charleston, SC 29401
(800) 622–INNS or (803) 723–8691
Rates: $98 to $200

"The" inn is actually five buildings, three restored single houses and two carriage houses clustered around a courtyard. Antiques and oriental rugs furnish the guest rooms, and paintings by one of the innkeepers, Lucille Mulholland, are hung throughout the inn. As the name of the inn implies, the

Mulhollands like things French. Many of Lucille's paintings evoke the work of the French Impressionists. At tea time, a bottle of French wine always accompanies the tea and sandwiches, and Christmas celebrations always include French traditions. You won't find another place quite like this in Charleston.

Continental breakfast is included in the rates.

The inn has fifteen rooms, including two suites, all with private bath, television, and telephone.

VENDUE INN
    19 Vendue Range
    Charleston, SC 29401
    (800) 845–7900 outside S.C.; (800) 922–7900 or (803)
    577–7970 inside S.C.
    Rates: $95 to $145 for rooms, $155 to $200 for suites.

This inn used to be an old warehouse. Its exposed old beams and worn pine floors play an important part in the decor. From the rooftop garden you have a fine view of Patriots Point and Fort Sumter. The guest rooms have canopied and poster beds and 18th century reproduction furniture. The inn's restaurant, The Library, has a cozy English library decor and serves excellent fresh seafood presented as artistically as good paintings.

Continental breakfast is included in the rates.

The inn has thirty-four rooms, all with private bath, television, and telephone. Some rooms have a Jacuzzi, some a fireplace, some a sitting area, some wheelchair access.

MILLS HOUSE HOTEL
    115 Meeting Street
    Charleston, SC 29401
    (803) 577–2400
    Rates: $95 to $155

The first Mills House Hotel on this site was built about 1853. The present hotel was patterned after the original Italianate building. It incorporates from the first hotel the iron balcony on which General Robert E. Lee stood in 1861 watching a huge fire rage through Charleston. The hotel's public rooms are elegant, with vast expanses of white marble and elaborate furnishings. Guest accommodations range from small rooms to good-sized suites.

The hotel has 215 rooms, all with private bath, some with refrigerators, all with television and telephone, some with wheelchair access. The hotel has a swimming pool, as well as a paid-parking garage.

Dining

If you can't find something you like to eat in Charleston, you probably don't like food. Although the area is especially famous for seafood and Lowcountry cooking, tourism and a well-traveled local population have led to increasing numbers of ethnic restaurants as well. You should understand that while Lowcountry cooking is Southern, all Southern cooking is definitely not Lowcountry. For example, hushpuppies are Southern; grits are (some say "is") Southern. She-crab soup is Lowcountry; sautéed shrimp with grits is Lowcountry. Probably the best approach is to stop worrying about what the food is called and concentrate on how it tastes.

BOCCI'S

158 Church Street at the corner of Church and Cumberland
(803) 720–2121
Open for lunch and dinner seven days a week.
All spirits available.

Coming upon Bocci's for the first time, people tend to believe that they have "discovered" it, and even a framed clipping on the wall calls it the "new kid on the block," but in fact this restaurant has been around a while. It has become well enough established to increase its operation from part of the week to every day. The place has become a favorite of local people who like good Italian food. The menu ranges from calzone and salads to such pasta specialties as fettuccini with shrimp and scallops topped with Parmesan cheese grated at your table.

The terra-cotta floor and bright clay-colored walls both lend an air of casualness to the place, heightening its Italian feel.

BOOKSTORE CAFE

Corner of King & Hutson Street
(803) 720–8843
Open for breakfast and lunch Monday through Friday.

There's a kind of simple inspiration to this little place around the corner from the Visitors Center. When you open the door to enter, you're greeted by the pleasant aromas of baked goods and coffee. The tables are small, with straight-backed chairs. Books about Charleston and Southern history cram shelves all around the room. You see at once that you're in a café where people thumb the books and unashamedly read newspapers at the table. Breakfast specialties range from standard eggs, grits, and toast to elaborate three-egg omelettes, bagels and cream cheese, and pancakes. In addition to coffee and tea, cappuccino, café au lait, and espresso are offered.

For lunch your choices include sandwiches, soups, and salads.

COLONY HOUSE

35 Prioleau Street at the Waterfront Park
(803) 723–3424
Open for lunch and dinner daily, Sunday brunch.
All spirits available.

The Colony House is said to be the oldest restaurant in Charleston, but renovation of the building has made the place look large and airy, rather like a garden room. The restaurant specializes in upscale Lowcountry cooking; the place is popular with local people for business and club lunches as well as with tourists.

The crabcakes are outstanding. Made with fresh crabmeat, of course, each serving is one very large patty with mild seasonings and little filler. The cakes are sautéed rather than fried. Appetizers include the ubiquitous she-crab soup, black bean soup, oyster pie, and pulled pork on corncakes. Pulled pork requires explanation. It is marinated roast pork pulled from the bone, shredded, and served over thin pan-fried corncakes. Steaks and chicken are available for those disinclined to eat Lowcountry food but willing to tag along with those who like it.

HYMAN'S SEAFOOD COMPANY
215 Meeting Street
(803) 723–0233
Open every day 11:00 A.M. to 11:00 P.M.
All spirits available.

For a huge number of moderately priced fresh seafood choices, try Hyman's. The restaurant sprawls in a big old warehouse where casual dress and families with children are perfectly appropriate. You can order complete seafood dinners fried, broiled, or blackened. Chicken and aged beef are also on the menu. Everything comes in generous portions. In the lounge and oyster bar on the second floor you can get raw oysters and drinks.

You may also order from the menu for Aaron's Deli, a traditional New York-style deli that is part of the same operation although it's in a different part of the building. The deli door opens at 213 Meeting street. Hours are 7:30 A.M. to 11 P.M. Phone (803) 723–6000.

LONGHORN STEAKS
61 State Street
(803) 577–4091
Open for lunch Monday through Saturday, dinner Monday through Sunday.
All spirits available.

At first it sounds crazy to go for steaks in what must be the seafood capital of South Carolina, but after several days of fish and Lowcountry specialties, the straightforward aroma of steaks being panfried can be wonderful. You'll find this a ca-

sual, easy place to eat when you want a good, basic steak dinner. But don't expect a salad bar because, as the sign on the
door says, "Some things are meant to be separate."

MAGIC WOK
    219 Meeting Street
    (803) 723–8163
    Open every day 11:00 A.M. to 10:00 P.M.
    Beer and wine available.

Your possibilities here range from a quick, simple lunch to a
multicourse dinner. Offerings range from fried rice to the
elaborate entrée "Seven Stars around the Moon," which contains lobster, scallops, pork, beef, chicken, and vegetables.
The menu also includes vegetarian choices and diet entrées
prepared with no oil, sugar, or salt. The cooks use no mono-
sodium glutamate in anything.

LE MIDI
    337 King Street
    (803) 577–5571
    Open for lunch Monday through Friday, dinner Monday
    through Saturday.
    All spirits available.

Try this restaurant for authentic classical French food
served in comfortable, unpretentious surroundings. The food
gets more emphasis than decor. Some examples: homemade
goose liver pâté, veal sweetbreads, duck with cherries, and
delicate baked caramel custard. Warm French bread and sweet
butter accompany all the entrées. The restaurant has a nice
wine list with some moderately priced choices.

PINCKNEY CAFE AND ESPRESSO
    18 Pinckney Street
    (803) 577–0961
    Open for lunch and dinner Tuesday through Saturday.
    Beer and wine available.

It takes a little looking to find this place, which refers to itself as a "New American Bistro." It's tucked into the first floor of an old frame house (and uses the porch too in good weather) at the corner of Pinckney Street and Motley Lane, two blocks north of the market. Old-fashioned flowers such as pansies, snapdragons, and calendula mingle casually with parsley plants along the edge of the walk. If you aren't looking for a restaurant, you could dismiss this as another house in an alley. That would be too bad.

The food and the mood recall the natural food restaurants and coffee houses of a generation or two past, but with a more sophisticated menu. You can drink red zinger tea or specialty coffees, eat Lowcountry duck soup with kale and turnip greens, or choose baked ziti with shrimp. Salads and sandwiches are available short-order. Bourbon peach cobbler is one popular dessert. The portions are generous. The clientele seems to include more local people than tourists, which is usually considered a sign of good food. The atmosphere is thoroughly relaxed, with a kind of noisy cheerfulness that echos from the bare old wood floors.

POOGAN'S PORCH
   68 Queen Street
   (803) 577–2337
   Open every day for lunch and dinner.
   All spirits available.

Poogan's has become an institution in Charleston. The restaurant was named for a dog left behind when his owners sold their house and moved away. The ownership of the restaurant changed several times, but Poogan remained as its mascot until he died in 1979. Recently the old home at 72 Queen Street burned, and now Poogan's spirit presides over the same Lowcountry food and Southern ambiance at 68 Queen, just a few doors away from the original location. This is a place for sampling gumbos, jambalayas, and crabmeat delicacies as well as a special treatment of Carolina quail. Or order chicken and beef when you feel less adventurous. The bread pudding with bourbon sauce and the peanut butter pie are two quintessentially Southern desserts. Somewhere, you just know it, Poogan approves.

PRIMROSE HOUSE
> 332 East Bay Street
> (803) 723–2954
> Open for lunch Monday through Friday, dinner Monday through Saturday, Sunday brunch.
> All spirits available.

Still something of a secret in Charleston, The Primrose offers some of the best, most innovative cooking anywhere in town. The chefs experiment with new ideas all the time. They use fresh vegetables, and many of their herbs and garnishes grow in the flower beds by the restored 1817 mansion that houses the basement restaurant. You'll always find interesting but not excessive treatments of fresh seafood here as well as original and tasty soups and appetizers. The crabcakes and salads are so good you could eat them every day.

RESTAURANT MILLION
> 2 Unity Alley
> (803) 577–7472
> Open Monday through Thursday 6:30 P.M. to 10:00 P.M., Friday and Saturday to 10:30 P.M. Reservations required.
> All spirits available.

Plan on dressing up, and expect to spend a lot of money. Restaurant Million goes all the way with a French menu (and English translation), wine suggestions, and impeccable formal service. Some examples of the food: braised veal sweetbreads with morel mushrooms, lightly breaded sea scallops layered with herb mousse, and Maine lobster fricassee with artichoke hearts. For dessert, perhaps puff pastry with caramel sauce or petits fours or profiteroles au chocolat. The specifics may change, but you get the idea. The restaurant is in a restored 1788 building. It takes some care to find it the first time. Unity Alley runs between 149 and 151 East Bay Street.

Day Trips

McClellanville

About 30 miles north of Charleston on US 17/701 at the edge of Francis Marion National Forest, this tiny spot attracted national attention when it was devastated by Hurricane Hugo in 1989. Since then, the people have slowly been rebuilding their lives and livelihoods. The little town, which is midway between Georgetown and Charleston, is a commercial fishing village. It's the kind of place you'd call picturesque if the buildings and streets were just a little more carefully groomed. As it is, you might call it authentic. Boating, hiking, and hunting in the nearby (storm-damaged) Francis Marion National Forest are still excellent.

The story of one tiny bed and breakfast operation, Village B & B, gives you insight into the spirit of the community. Cheri and Matthew George's pretty little one-room bed and breakfast, attached to their home by a breezeway, was a beautiful place with an old Southern pine floor, fluffy white and peach beds, and a breakfast area by a big window. During Hurricane Hugo, water from the Atlantic Ocean pushed in, floating the family's home and the inn completely off their foundations. The Georges hauled the buildings back onto their foundations. Everyone scrubbed and patched and painted until they had everything back the way it had been and they could return to business as usual.

One part of "business as usual" may be especially appealing to you if you're interested in realistic art. Matthew George works in construction for a living. In his spare time he paints—not houses, pictures. Occasionally you can find some of his work in a gallery somewhere in the area, but most of his oils, watercolors, and prints are on display in the B & B, matted and protected in vinyl. The bins and walls are filled with seascapes and paintings of local outdoor scenes, birds, flowers, and shells.

The work is modestly priced. It has elicited praise from framers who have seen it when the Georges' guests returned home with pictures to be framed. Staying at the Village B & B and buying some paintings is fun. Matthew's back supply was ruined by the hurricane, but he started over and keeps going strong. The Georges would welcome the opportunity to show you Matthew's work even if you aren't spending the night, but it's important to call ahead at (803) 887–3266.

Summerville

Situated twenty-three miles northwest of Charleston on SC 165, this town gets its name from its origin: it began as a summer place primarily for the wealthy rice planters around Charleston who wanted to escape the coastal heat and the threat of malaria. They built their "cottages" up off the ground for protection from dampness and pests, and they established a tradition of protecting and replanting trees that remains a priority, especially since the destruction caused by Hurricane Hugo in 1989.

When you get into Summerville, stop at the Chamber of Commerce, 106 East Doty Avenue (803–873–2931), for brochures about the area, including "Wandering Historic Summerville" (a walking tour with notes about what you'll see), "Discovering Dorchester County," and guides to antiques and crafts shops in town. The Chamber people can also tell you about the spring flower festival, which is scheduled as closely as possible to coincide with the blooming of the azaleas (usually late March-early April; the exact dates change from year to year) and attracts 250,000 visitors. Another festival is "A Taste of Summerville," for which the town's restaurants prepare some of their specialties. If you want to write in advance about these activities, mail your letter to the address above; the zip is 29483.

Speaking of restaurants, a good one to try is Froggy's (104 East Doty Avenue; 803–873–3763), which is located next-door to the Chamber of Commerce in the old icehouse, a building in which ice was actually made a hundred years ago. Froggy's is open for lunch Tuesday through Friday and for dinner Tuesday through Saturday. In addition to its trademark frog legs, Froggy's offerings include steak, seafood, bacon-wrapped scallops, deep-sea pasta, steamer pots, lobster pots, and a marinated rotisseried chicken. All spirits are available.

Another place to eat in Summerville is BoJo's Seafood, at 114 Central Avenue (803–875–3357), open for lunch Sunday through Friday 11:30 A.M. to 2:30 P.M. and for dinner Wednesday through Saturday 5:00 P.M. to 10:00 P.M. BoJo's specializes in just what you'd expect from its name and is particularly proud of its scallops, seafood platter, and daily specials. Beer and wine are available here.

You can combine a visit to Summerville very nicely with visits to Drayton Hall, Magnolia Plantation and Gardens, and Middleton Place (see pages 25, 26, and 27, respectively). If you'd like to spend the night here, you might try the Bed and Breakfast of Summerville, 304 South Hampton Street (Summerville, SC 29483; phone 803–871–5275). It's located in the historic district and offers accommodations in the restored dependency, or outbuilding, which looks like a little Williamsburg house. It has a fireplace and an equipped kitchen. The cottage has a sofa bed, stretching the sleeping space to accommodate four people. Rates, depending on season, number of people, and whether or not you want a continental breakfast included, are from $40 to $50.

Another bed and breakfast is Gadsden Manor, 329 Old Postern Road, Summerville, SC 29483; phone (803) 875–2602. This is an early 1900s mansion in a Summerville suburb just a mile from downtown. It has nine rooms with private bath and one suite; rates are from $65 to $70 for rooms and $89.50 for the suite, including continental breakfast.

BEAUFORT

Beaufort (pronounced "BEW fort") is an engaging little sea-port town about an hour south of Charleston, close to the Georgia border. The second-oldest town in South Carolina, settled in 1711, it's the kind of place people inevitably call pic-turesque and sleepy, and its main business these days is tour-ism. But for all its placid appearance, you'll find a lot of fun and a lot of history waiting to be discovered there.

The history seems to have been mostly fighting and facing adversity. The action dates back to the landing of a Spanish sea captain in 1514, leading to the establishment of a Spanish fort about a decade later. Most of its men died during their first winter.

In 1562 the French attempted a Protestant settlement in the area, but after their captain went back to France for supplies, the rest of the men soon gave up and, with help from the In-dians, built a ship and sailed away too.

Then the Spanish took another turn, destroying the existing fort and using the area as a central point for their own explo-rations.

In 1670 a British colony stayed for a while before moving on to settle Charles Town. The Scots came in 1684, lasting only a couple of years before being undone by the Spaniards.

Officially, the town of Beaufort was laid out in 1710 and formally established by charter from the Lords Proprietors a year later. It was named for Lord Proprietor Henry, Duke of Beaufort. Despite all this officialdom, the town barely sur-vived attacks just five years later by the Yemassee Indians.

There's more. Beaufort was conquered by the British in the Revolution and threatened by their gunboats in the war of 1812.

When the Civil War began, the men of Beaufort took off to serve in the Confederate forces, and soon afterwards their families fled, leaving the town occupied by Union soldiers. This occupation probably saved Beaufort from being burned to the ground by Sherman's troops as were all the other towns between Savannah, Georgia, and Fayetteville, North Carolina.

What you find today as a sightseer is that most of the old homes in Beaufort are either fairly modest pre-Revolutionary buildings or more elaborate antebellum homes of the 1800s, graced with old live oaks, wisteria, and flowers blooming nearly year-round. The oldest home is the Thomas Hepworth House, circa 1717, on New Street.

Activities and Attractions

VISITOR INFORMATION CENTER

Greater Beaufort Chamber of Commerce, on the waterfront at 1006 Bay Street
(803) 524–3163
Open Monday through Saturday 9:30 A.M. to 5:30 P.M., Sunday 10:00 A.M. to 5:00 P.M. Tours leave from the Visitor Information Center on the hour from 9:00 A.M. to 4:00 P.M. Each tour lasts about 45 minutes.
Admission $8.50 for adults, $4.50 for children.

Make your first stop in Beaufort here. The staff function competently and enthusiastically, passing out walking tour maps, marking points of particular interest for you, and offering suggestions for restaurants and lodging. They can also tell you about spring and fall tours of private residences and other annual events.

The town tour map shows twenty-six historical sites including houses, gardens, St. Helena's Episcopal Church (1724), the Baptist Church of Beaufort (1844), and the George Elliott House Museum (circa 1840), which was a federal hospital during the Civil War. Notes about each site are printed on the back of the map. An entertaining way to take in the local history is in a horse-drawn carriage driven by a professional guide.

PENN CENTER HISTORIC DISTRICT
P.O. Box 126
Frogmore, SC 29920
Lands End Road on St. Helena Island
(803) 838–2432
Museum open daily.

Penn Center, founded in 1862 by Northern missionaries, was the first school established in the South to educate freed slaves. Now a living history museum situated on forty-nine acres of land, it encompasses sixteen buildings including cottages and dormitories for groups of up to 100 people. It has a small museum focusing on the language, history, and culture of the blacks who were native to this region. It also has an outstanding community outreach program. Penn Center was designated a National Historic Landmark in 1974. Write or call ahead to get information on accommodations and special annual events.

PARRIS ISLAND MUSEUM
Parris Island, SC 29905
(803) 525–2951
The island is open Monday through Friday 7:00 A.M. to 4:30 P.M.; Saturday, Sunday, and holidays 9:00 A.M. to 4:30 P.M. The museum is open Monday through Saturday 10:00 A.M. to 4:30 P.M., Thursday to 7:00 P.M. To arrange tours, call during the same hours.
Admission free.

With so much military activity having transpired in the area, it isn't surprising that Parris Island should be a popular attraction. It's an active Marine Corps base more oriented to tourists than most military bases are. Visitors may take a driving tour of the island through the old Navy Yard, to the site of the Spanish forts, and past training areas.

The museum exhibits in the War Memorial Building show the history and development of Parris Island and the Marine Corps.

HUNTING ISLAND STATE PARK
1775 Sea Island Parkway
(16 miles east of Beaufort on US 21)
St. Helena Island, SC 29920
(803) 838–2011 or (803) 838–2152

When you've had it with history and just want to play, the place to go is Hunting Island, a 5,000-acre state park with three miles of swimming beaches, public boat-launch points, fishing reefs, and hiking and nature trails. As you hike through nearly tropical greenery you'll see many small game animals, birds, and giant sea turtles, protected now because hunting is no longer allowed.

The beach is one of the best in the Southeast for shelling. For a panoramic view, you can climb the 181 steps to the top of the Hunting Island Lighthouse (open from noon until dusk every day), near the public swimming beach. The lighthouse was built in 1859 and has stood in several different locations as erosion has changed the shape of the island.

Camping facilities for trailers and tents for stays of up to a week are available on the island, but you can't make reservations; it's strictly a first-come arrangement. You can reserve rental cabins, but you need to do it early because the park often has a waiting list. Write the address above or call the above telephone number.

Lodging

RHETT HOUSE
1009 Craven Street
Beaufort, SC 29902
(803) 524–9030
Rates: $95 to $175

This inn, with wraparound verandas, classic columns and porticos, and beautifully carved entry stairs, has attracted such celebrities as Barbara Streisand and Nick Nolte, who were in Beaufort during the filming of *The Prince of Tides*, as well as the regular tourist trade. Two of the rooms have fireplaces. Rates for commoners and famous folk alike include breakfast. Dinner is available by special arrangement.

TWO-SUNS INN
  1705 Bay Street
  Beaufort, SC 29902
  (800) 532–4244 or (803) 522–1122
  Rates: $85 to $93; one suite for $168

Try bed and breakfast accommodations in a restored Neoclassical Revival-style home which once served as a communal home for female teachers in Beaufort. An interesting feature here is the colorful weaving studio of innkeeper Carrol Kay, in the front room to the right of the entrance.

BEST WESTERN SEA ISLAND
  1015 Bay Street
  Beaufort, SC 29902
  (800) 528–1234 or (803) 522–2090
  Rates: $63–$84

Dining

BANANA'S
  910 Bay Street
  (803) 522–0910
  Open 11:30 A.M. to 10:00 P.M. every day but Monday.
  All spirits available.

They call themselves "the fun spot on the waterfront." It's true. You're appropriately dressed in shorts and tee shirts or jeans. The menu features such snack foods as hot buffalo wings and homemade potato chips. Banana's serves at least eight different sandwiches, a couple of different hot dogs, and nine kinds of half-pound burgers. You don't really need it, but three-bean salad accompanies them. You can order steaks, ribs, fresh fish, or shrimp for more substantial meals. Salad, vegetables, potato, and homemade bread go with the entrées. There's entertainment on weekends.

GADSBY RESTAURANT
    822 Bay Street
    (803) 525–1800
    Open Monday through Thursday 11:30 A.M. to 9:30 P.M.,
    Friday and Saturday until 10:00 P.M. Closed Sunday.
    All spirits available.

The restaurant is part of the Gadsby Tavern, named for an inn run by John Gadsby from 1796 to 1808 in Alexandria, Virginia, that was a social center for federal dignitaries. George Washington made his farewell address to his troops from its front steps. The Gadsby Tavern in Beaufort was begun by direct descendents of John Gadsby. It's settled back among live oaks draped with Spanish moss on the Beaufort River. The dining room terrace overlooks the river. The restaurant specializes in fresh local seafood served steamed, broiled, fried in delicate batter, or on a cold seafood plate. Prices are moderate. For instance, you can order a dinner of fresh flounder stuffed with crab for less than $10.

HILTON HEAD

Local people say "Hilton HEAD." Closer to Savannah than Charleston, located between the Intracoastal Waterway and the Atlantic Ocean, Hilton Head is a twelve-mile-long island that has been developed into nearly wall-to-wall resorts, tennis courts, golf courses, lodgings, eateries, shops, and condos. Writing a guide to Hilton Head would be a lot like writing one for Las Vegas. But it wasn't always that way.

Several thousand years ago, Indians lived here. Experts disagree on exactly how *many* thousand years ago, but it could be as many as four. The Indians successfully prevented settlement attempts by the Spanish, French, and English until the middle of the 1700s. Then British planters brought in indigo, cotton, and rice and did well with these crops until the Civil War. After the war, without slaves to work the crops, the planters left the island. The freed slaves lived basically rural lives in what is known now as the Gullah culture. The Gullah life-style is best known for savory Lowcountry cooking based on seafood, vegetables, and rice. Less familiar, the Gullah language, which sounds nearly like English with the words in different order, leaves you feeling that you *almost* understand what you're hearing.

As the island's balmy climate and beautiful beaches began to attract developers, the black people and their Gullah traditions were gradually squeezed out. When the bridge from the island to the mainland was completed in the late 1950s, development of the island as a vacation spot increased, eradicating even more of what it once was.

But as a resort area, Hilton Head still has its charm. The climate is semitropical, except for an occasional peculiar winter when you find snow on the beaches. The beaches are of the same gentle slope and fine white sand as the Grand Strand farther north on the mainland. Hilton Head's beaches and balmy climate attract visitors by the thousands — by the fifty thousands. During peak vacation periods, the base island population of about 20,000 swells by as many as 55,000 more people. The off-season comes in winter, November to March. That's a great time to visit the island if you don't like crowds. It may not be warm enough to swim, but, depending on the winter, you may very well bicycle on the beaches in shorts. And you can golf, play tennis, and shop all year.

Before you decide where to stay and what to do on Hilton Head, and surely before you try to find your way around, you should contract the Hilton Head Island Visitor and Conventions Bureau, P.O. Box 5647, Hilton Head Island, SC 29938 (803–785–3673 or 800–523–3373) for brochures and a map of the island.

Activities and Attractions

Hilton Head has beautiful beaches not only for swimming but also for walking; you can go literally for miles on foot and enjoy looking at some of the oceanfront homes as you do. It's fun too to walk along the residential streets close to the beaches to see the homes. Their variety and the taste with which they are landscaped make for a good morning of sightseeing. Biking trails will also get you into some of the residential areas and into more natural areas as well. Bird-watching is great — Audubon Society members have reported seeing more than 120 species on the island.

Shopping is another favorite activity of visitors. You can find something for everyone here, from fine antiques to mundane souvenir items. Your information from the Visitor and Conventions Bureau — or several free publications you can pick up at many locations on the island — will give you a rundown of the shops and malls.

Listed below are a few specific attractions.

HARBOUR TOWN
    Lighthouse Lane
    Sea Pines Plantation
    Open daily year-round; restaurants and shops have varying
    hours.

This group of upscale shops, restaurants, and condominiums wraps around a ninety-three-slip yacht basin used by serious boaters who travel the Intracoastal Waterway. The cove and lighthouse appear in many photos of Hilton Head. You can spend a lot of time just watching boats. In the restaurants you can get a fancy meal or just an ice-cream cone. If you'd like to do nothing but soak up the atmosphere, it's okay to sit in a rocker on the terrace outside the shops and watch the people come and go; you'll see quite an assortment. Play areas and special entertainment programs are provided for children. Inquire here about boat tours to Dafuskie Island, which you can see from Harbour Town on a clear day.

SOUTH BEACH MARINA VILLAGE
    South Sea Pines Drive to South Beach
    Sea Pines Plantation
    Open daily year-round. Restaurants, shops, and activities
    have varying hours.

You may think you're in New England when you get here, especially if you arrive when the sycamores are turning in the fall. The area offers shops, casual and formal dining, boat rentals, sailing lessons, wind surfing, deep-sea fishing, cruises, swimming and tennis, and a playground for children.

SEA PINES FOREST PRESERVE
    Greenwood Drive and Lawton Road
    Open daily from daylight to dusk year-round.

You can walk or ride the trails on horseback through this 605-acre wildlife refuge. One of its attractions is the Indian Shell Ring, which is believed to date back to 1450 BC and is made of more than 50,000 bushels of oyster shells, animal bones, and pottery fragments. Its use is unknown, but it's fun to speculate about. You'll find fishing ponds and a picnic area here too. Self-guided maps for walking through the preserve are available at the entrance. Be prepared for mosquitoes and other insects in the forest during the warmest months.

LAWTON STABLES
Greenwood Drive
Sea Pines Plantation
(803) 671–2586
Open daily year-round.

Here you can start on a professionally guided trail ride through the Sea Pines Forest Preserve, arrange a special ride for children 8 and up, or treat smaller children to a pony ride. Call for rates and schedules.

BAYARD RUINS
Bayard Park Road
Sea Pines Plantation
Open daily daylight to dusk year-round.

The foundation walls here are made of tabby, a material consisting of crushed oyster shells and sand, and they're all that's left of a plantation house that was built in 1800 and burned during the Civil War.

WHOOPING CRANE CONSERVANCY
Off US 278 in Hilton Head Plantation
Open daily dawn to dusk September through February.
Closed March through August for nesting season.
Admission free. Explain at the gate to Hilton Head
Plantation where you are going.

A self-guided tour along a boardwalk and nature trail will take you into this 137-acre nature preserve, where you can see many species of waterfowl and other birds, along with mammals and small reptiles. You can also join an hour-long bird walk at 9:00 A.M. on Saturdays.

LOWCOUNTRY FACTORY OUTLET VILLAGE
US 278 at the Gateway to Hilton Head Island
(803) 837–4339
Open Monday through Saturday 10:00 A.M. to 9 P.M.,
Sunday noon to 6:00 P.M.

This place claims to be the area's largest outlet shopping center, with more than forty brand-name merchants represented, including J. Crew, Young Generations, Eddie Bauer, and Danskin.

Golf and Tennis

Many people come here for these sports. Here again you should get full information from the Visitor and Conventions Bureau, listed above. Below are just a few of several possibilities for places to play. Call for rates and other information.

HARBOUR TOWN GOLF LINKS
Lighthouse Lane
Sea Pines Plantation
(803) 671–4417

This course, which *Sports Illustrated* called "nothing short of a work of art," is host to the annual MCI Heritage Classic and has been played by Arnold Palmer, Jack Nicklaus, and other golf greats.

SHIPYARD GOLF CLUB
Off Shipyard Drive in Shipyard Plantation
(803) 785–2402

This twenty-seven-hole course makes its way through Shipyard, offering looks at some of the development's houses and villas and a view of the lagoon. The course was designed by George Cobb and Willard Byrd.

SEA PINES RACQUET CLUB
Lighthouse Road
(803) 671–2494

This Harbour Town club has twenty-five clay courts and five hard courts. The courts are lighted. Tennis lessons and intensive training are available here. Guests of Sea Pines receive some free time on the courts.

PALMETTO DUNES/ROD LAVER TENNIS
Queen's Folly Road in Palmetto Dunes Resort
(803) 785–1152

This facility offers twenty-five courts with three surfaces to choose from. Courts are lighted. Guests of the resort may play free.

Lodging

Possibilities for lodging on Hilton Head are almost broader than the island. They range from smaller motels to condos of various sizes to very large private homes for rent. Where you should stay depends on how much space you need, what kind of surroundings you want, what recreational facilities you'd like to have close by, and how much you want to pay. Therefore, you won't find any specific recommendations in this section, just general advice.

Four major resort communities dominate the island. They are Sea Pines Plantation (803–785–3333), Palmetto Dunes (800–845–6130), Port Royal Plantation (803–681–4000), and Shipyard Plantation (803–842–2400). All offer not only lodging but shopping, dining, and recreational activities. Each has its own charms.

Sea Pines, located at the western tip of the island, is the oldest, and it charges $3.00 a day per car for admission into its gates. If you are staying in Sea Pines, your hotel or condominium office will provide a free pass for the duration of your visit. Since Sea Pines has many special attractions, having the free pass may be a factor in your decision about where to stay, especially if you plan to be on the island for several days.

Port Royal Plantation is definitely upscale and has three championship golf courses and a choice of clay, grass, and hard courts for tennis. Shipyard Plantation is oriented toward families and has many condos for rent. It also has three nine-hole golf courses and a racquet club.

There are also many places to stay that aren't in these four resort communities.

Besides the general information you'll get from the Visitor and Conventions Bureau, listed above, you can get specific information on accommodations available when you plan to visit from Hilton Head Central Reservations, Box 5312, Hilton Head Island, SC 29938; phone (800) 845–7018. They answer the phone casually, "Hilton Head Central," but they know what's going on. If you explain your needs and price range, they can suggest where to stay as well as when and how to get the best rates.

Dining

You can get just about any kind of food imaginable here, from fast to fancy. Pick up a free restaurant guide when you arrive. Below are just a few suggestions.

TRUFFLES CAFE
    Sea Pines Center on Lighthouse Road
    (803) 671–6136
    Open daily for lunch and dinner.
    All spirits available.

Soups, sandwiches, and salads are excellent here. So are the French dough pizzas and grilled Cajun chicken. All ingredients are fresh, servings are attractive, and the decor is casual and welcoming. A specialty food market sells freshly baked goods and deli items.

Café Europa

> At the Lighthouse in Harbour Town
> (803) 671–3399
> Open daily for breakfast 10:00 A.M. to 11:30 A.M., lunch 11:00 A.M. to 2:30 P.M., and dinner 5:30 P.M. to 10:00 P.M.
> All spirits available.

Besides fresh fish entrées, you'll find chicken, duckling, veal, and steaks on the menu. Something more out of the ordinary is the shrimp and sausage salad that's served for lunch and the desserts that are made on the spot. Here you can be casual and enjoy the view of the harbor and Calibogue Sound. Sometimes it gets crowded; reservations are suggested for dinner.

Harbour Town Grill

> Lighthouse Lane in Harbour Town
> (803) 671–3119
> Open daily for breakfast, lunch, and dinner.
> All spirits available.

This small restaurant is in the clubhouse for the Harbour Town Golf Links and looks out onto the course. Its decor features portraits of Heritage champions. Items on the dinner menu include lamb, fresh fish, veal, prime rib, and steaks. For elegance, this is it. At dinner the waiters wear tuxedos, the tables are candlelit, and fresh flowers are all around. Jackets are suggested at night, and reservations are recommended.

MYRTLE BEACH

To understand Myrtle Beach now, you need to know what it used to be like. Only a few decades ago it was a slow-moving beach town visited mostly by South Carolinians looking for a few low-key days of sea and sun. The fine white-sand beaches were broad and flat, easing gently into the surf. Folks stayed in summer cottages and at modest hotels. Local people ran a few concessions and some home-style restaurants. In the 1920s, an elegant resort for the well-to-do flourished here until the Great Depression, but it wasn't until the 1960s that Myrtle Beach became known nationally as a resort. Another surge of growth came in the 1980s.

Since then Myrtle Beach has continued its boom to become a full-scale resort area. It attracts a yearly pilgrimage of Canadians, beginning in early March for spring vacation (Canadians don't like heat), in sufficient numbers to warrant breaking out the "Welcome Canadians" greetings at every hotel, motel, and restaurant with a marquee. It is the destination of choice every June for thousands of graduating high school seniors, who arrive under the motto "Myrtle or Bust" for a week of revelry.

For older people, it has become a popular retirement spot. The increasing number of retirees earned the area the nickname Miami North from folks who were happier when Myrtle Beach was just a sleepy spot on the beach. As recently as 1950 the permanent population of Myrtle Beach wasn't much over 3,000. Now it's more than eight times that, largely supporting the tourist industry. At the peak of the summer, if you count the tourists, the population soars to about 350,000.

More people means more of everything else. Golf courses number more than seventy. Pro and amateur golf flourish, with tennis and racquet clubs running a close second. Major outlet shopping attracts thousands every day of the year. Large RV centers bring in motor homes and vacation trailers, individually and in caravans. Campers pitch tents on about 12,000 campsites spread among more than a dozen camp-grounds. A new marina condo slightly to the north has be-come a showplace for yachts. So many hotels, motels, and restaurants advertise that the giveaway guides are thicker than some science fiction novels. Rows of amusements and beach shops fill the downtown area and sprawl along the highway going north and south. In short, within easy memory of middle-aged people, Myrtle Beach has gone from small-town holiday spot to major commercial resort area. That's one change.

The other involves the beaches. Myrtle Beach sits at the cen-ter of the Grand Stand, a sixty-mile long stretch of beaches uninterrupted by tidal inlets. But natural erosion and hurri-canes have chewed away at those once-broad beaches, nar-rowing them to the point of threatening oceanfront properties. Sand is hauled in regularly as part of a beach nour-ishment process.

Since the ferocity of Hurricane Hugo in 1989 it hasn't been possible to restore all beaches to their earlier width, but they are still clean and appealing. Many slope gently into the water and make nice play areas for little children. A few spots of steeper beach decline produce waves robust enough to appeal to young would-be surfers.

For all the changes, something of the friendly spirit of the old days remains. A waitress or desk clerk who has dealt with hundreds of people before seeing you is still likely to share a giggle about the boss's plaid golf slacks or find you an aspirin if you complain of a headache. As for their beaches, local peo-ple are as proud of them as ever. The Strand may not be as it once was, but you still have to go far to find any beaches that are nicer, they'll say.

Even if you don't ordinarily enjoy developed vacation spots, you can, if you are willing to suspend your indignation at commercialism just slightly and enjoy the human touches where you find them, have a lot of fun at Myrtle Beach.

After all, you don't have to play miniature golf, although, given choices ranging from dinosaur land to medieval castles, it seems too good a piece of fantasy to skip altogether. Your taste may run more to the championship golf courses of the area, which, in their way, represent another sort of fantasy.

Activities and Attractions

In addition to beaches, miniature golf, and carnival-type amusements, Myrtle Beach has a number of attractions for good holiday fun.

Myrtle Waves Water Park

US 17 Bypass at 10th Avenue North
(803) 448–1026
Open from 10:00 A.M. daily Memorial Day through Labor Day. Closing times vary. Call for details.
Admission $8.95 for adults, $4.95 for children under forty-five inches tall.

In this twenty-acre park the theme obviously is water. More than eighteen water activities operate, including several different water slides and rides, a wave pool, and a children's wading pool. You can buy food at a café, and there are also concession stands, a gift shop, and an arcade. The admission price includes locker rooms with showers.

Waccatee Zoological Farm

8500 Enterprise Road, Myrtle Beach (Socastee) between the Intracoastal Waterway and SC 707. The turn for Enterprise Road is about half a mile west of SC 544 on SC 707.
(803) 650–8500
Admission $2.00

Unlike many area attractions, this one is open every day year-round. Kathleen Futrell says, "We have to be here to feed the animals every day, so we just stay open."

The zoo doesn't get a lot of publicity or buy a lot of advertising, so it's better known to local folks than to tourists. It's a special place. The farm started when Kathleen and her husband Archie, who say they "simply love animals," decided it would be fun to raise a lion. They bottle fed a female lion and had such good luck they were soon raising a male lion on a bottle too. That meant that pretty soon little lions came along. After that, the Futrells picked up deer and other animals in their travels. They found Chico, a chimpanzee, in Houston. He was their first member of the ape family and remains a favored pet. The Futrells continued traveling and bringing home animals they liked for more than a decade. The zoo finally opened to the public in 1988 because they got so many requests from schools and children's organizations to give tours. The Waccatee Zoo is on a 500-acre farm in Socastee, where more than 100 animals species are represented, from goats and pigs to leopards and chimpanzees, along with miniature pigs, cougars, even ostriches. Although fences and pens separate visitors and some animals, this is a place with no concrete or macadam. You can walk around in the open, exploring three trails, including a natural trail along which alligators, birds, and turtles have lived for at least four generations.

Inside a large cedar building that is heated in winter, you'll find monkeys chattering, exotic birds making their unique calls, and snakes being blessedly silent. A petting zoo holds animals especially raised to be safe for children.

OUTLET PARK AT WACCAMAW

> US 17 Bypass to SC 501 to the Intracoastal Waterway,
> between Conway and Myrtle Beach
> (803) 448–1573
> Open daily year-round.

The outlet park calls itself "a city of shopping." More than 100 stores in the complex sell brand-name merchandise — shoes, clothing, luggage, books, cosmetics, etc. — at discount prices. The Waccamaw Pottery, at the heart of the park, looks as big as a metropolitan airport (actually, it's a bit more than the size of five football fields) and has enough variety and volume in housewares and decorator's items to paralyze all but the most intrepid shopper. Within the malls you can buy light foods as well as beer and sit at café-style tables to consume them. The Waccamaw Train shuttles shoppers from one mall to another.

BAREFOOT LANDING
US 17 at North Myrtle Beach
Most of the shops and restaurants are open seven days a week. Some do not open until 1:00 P.M. Sundays.
Phone for cruise information: (803) 272–7743.

Barefoot Landing is a planned shopping complex vaguely reminiscent of the early days of Reston, Virginia, probably because of the architectural use of water and wood and the harmonious design of a planned complex. Boardwalks meander across grassy areas and large areas of water. Ducks occasionally float by.

If the appeal of the Waccamaw malls is bargain hunting, the appeal at Barefoot Landing is atmosphere. The shops and restaurants are built of weathered-looking wood and brightened with green awnings. Park benches along the boardwalks invite chatting and duck watching when you get tired of shopping. The shops are mostly the upscale gift and food shops, clothing stores, and boutiques typical of resort areas. The restaurants range in offerings from burgers to seafood and cocktails.

Children can ride a handpainted European-style carousel. At night pinpoints of light from the shops and boardwalk reflect on the water, making it a cool, pleasant place to stroll after dinner.

Cruises on the Intracoastal Waterway aboard the Barefoot Princess paddlewheel party boat leave from here. These include dining and entertainment. The cruises are so popular that during busy holidays they operate on a first-come basis; other times reservations are welcome. If you have your heart set on a cruise, it's important to call ahead.

Myrtle Beach State Park

US 17, 3 miles south of Myrtle Beach
(803) 238–5325
The park is open daily from 6:00 A.M. to 10:00 P.M. year-round.
Modest fees for day use; moderate fees for camping and cabins. Call for information and reservations.

This state park offers a nice combination of open beach and shaded, grassy picnic areas; one store where you pick up general supplies; and another, at the site of the old fishing pier destroyed by Hurricane Hugo, where you can get bait and tackle. The swimming pool is open from Memorial day through Labor day. There are lifeguards at the beach and pool during the summer.

The park was built by the Civilian Conservation Corps and shows the sturdy construction typical of CCC projects. The park comprises 312 acres, a hundred of which are maritime forest kept as a nature preserve. You can walk a nature trail with interpretive signs to learn about the plants and animals indigenous to the area.

For human needs, there are 350 camping sites and such attendant facilities as showers, restrooms, and laundry. A few cabins and apartments are also available.

To some visitors the noise of aircraft from the Myrtle Beach Air Force Base, across the highway from the park, seems incongruous in such a natural setting. However, by the time you visit, the base may be closed.

Carolina Opry, Dixie Jubilee, and Southern Country Nights

Carolina Opry is at 8901 Business US 17 North. Dixie Jubilee is at 701 Main, North Myrtle Beach. Southern Country Nights is at the old site of the Carolina Opry, south of Myrtle Beach at Surfside just off Business US 17. Request full directions when you make reservations.
Phone for all three shows: (803) 249–4444.
Show schedules vary. You need a reservation to get in. If one

show is sold out, the operators will let you know if
reservations are still open at the others.
Admission to Carolina Opry $12.95, $13.95, $14.96 for
adults, depending on how close to the stage you sit; $6.50
for children 3–11; free for children under 3 on parent's lap.
Dixie Jubilee and Southern Country Nights $12.95 for
adults, $6.50 for children 3–11, free for children under 3 on
parent's lap.

These are live musical variety shows featuring country and
pop music along with classic vaudeville routines, popular in-
spirational songs, and a rousing patriotic ending. It's God,
Mother, apple pie, and the flag; to have a good time you have
to slough off any cloak of sophistication you ordinarily wear.
If you can find refreshment in laughing until tears roll down
your face even though you know the old jokes are corny, and
in letting your emotions be tugged by what you ordinarily
consider sentimentalism, it's worth suspending judgment for a
couple of hours to become simply part of the audience.

The shows are one of the biggest success stories in town.
The drive behind them is Calvin Gilmore, an Ozark Mountain
farm boy whose love of country music led him to spend all the
money he earned working at Myrtle Beach one summer while
he was in college to buy a Gibson J–45 guitar. (Probably you
should pronounce that "GUI tar".) He turned out to be an
even better entrepreneur than musician. Carolina Opry made
its first performance in 1986. Audiences quickly filled the
house every night, leading Gilmore to begin the Dixie Jubilee
in 1989. It too plays to packed houses. The newest show is
Southern Country Nights, as popular as the others. In the audience, people who regularly see all the shows quibble about
which is best, but in fact the three are pretty much the same
except for having different performers and music.

The theaters are high-tech, state-of-the-art; the costumes
(designed by Gilmore's wife, Janis) are spectacular. The performers are energetically talented and radiate enthusiasm.
Some of them come from other professional theater back-
ground; some are natives of the coastal area; and all of them
are professional musicians. At the end of one show a member

of the audience asked one of the singers where she was from. "I'm from here, now," the singer said.

Between acts and at the end of the show, performers sit on the edge of the stage to talk to anyone—friends, fans, or family—who is interested. It's not uncommon to hear a singer asking someone in the audience how his mama's gettin' along or to see a bunch of kids coming front to greet their sister's best friend, the country singer.

Golf

Choosing the best courses from Myrtle Beach's offerings would be like trying to choose the best basket of apples at a farmers' market. They've all got good spots and bad spots, and it depends on what you like anyhow. The following public courses may serve as a starting point. For a complete current list of all golf courses in the area with details about playing them, contact the Myrtle Beach Area Chamber of Commerce, (803) 626–7444.

Tidewater Golf Club and Plantation
4901 Little River Neck Road
North Myrtle Beach, SC 29582
(800) 446–5363 or (803) 249–3829

In 1990, *Golf Digest* called this the best new public course in America. It is on a peninsula overlooking the Intracoastal Waterway and the Atlantic Ocean.

Legends
P.O. Box 65
North Myrtle Beach, SC 29597
(803) 236–9318

The Legends consists of three relatively new courses—the Heathland, the Moorland, and the Parkland—as well as a thirty-acre practice facility, a Scottish-style clubhouse, a golf museum, a club maker's shop, a restaurant, a pro shop, and a pub. William Price Fox, writer-in-residence at the University of South Carolina and author of many golfing articles, says in his book *Golfing in the Carolinas* that the Heathland reminds him of a difficult, windy course in Dublin. Fox may or may not be the most expert judge of golf courses in the area, but he has the distinction of being one golfer who is willing to put his opinions into print for all to test.

MYRTLE BEACH HILTON ARCADIAN SHORE GOLF CLUB
701 Hilton Road
Myrtle Beach, SC 29577
(803) 449–5000

This is another course Fox includes in his book as outstanding. It was designed by Rees Jones, and, Fox says, is a combination of a good modern layout and a great natural setting. If you stay at the Hilton, the hotel will arrange tee times for you at this and/or other area courses.

MYRTLE BEACH NATIONAL GOLF CLUB
P.O. Box 1936
Myrtle Beach, SC 29578
(800) 334–5590 or (803) 448–2308

This well-established club, built in 1973, has three courses: The North Course, the West Course, and Southcreek. Arnold Palmer designed the North Course, and the other two are said to reflect his preferences in golfing.

Lodging

In a resort where hotels and motels run practically wall to wall, recommending any particular ones requires audacity. Myrtle Beach has a full complement of Holiday Inn, Best Western, Hyatt and mom-and-pop types of accommodations. For a list long enough to cover the boardwalk, contact the Myrtle Beach Area Chamber of Commerce, P.O. Box 2115 AG-H/M, Myrtle Beach, SC 29578–2115. Phone (800)

356–3016 or (803) 626–7444. In addition, here are a handful of special places to try.

CHESTERFIELD INN
> 700 North Ocean Boulevard
> Myrtle Beach, SC 29578
> (803) 448–3177
> Rates: $60 to $128 including breakfast and dinner, $22 to $95 without meals
> Closed December and January.

When you ask the people around Myrtle Beach about "unusual accommodations," they answer, "Chesterfield Inn" without a pause. Nothing else like it exists here. The Chesterfield is an old-fashioned beachfront hotel, brick and wood rather than chrome and plastic, only three stories high. The rooms are comfortable but simply furnished. The lobby looks like a big family den or the greatroom of a country lodge. The dining room has wood paneling and terra-cotta floors with a wall of big windows through which you see a rocker-lined porch fronting on a well-tended lawn, which connects the porch to the beach.

The same stability you see in the building marks the staff. Clay Brittain, the previous innkeeper, was associated with the place from the time he started working summers, in 1945, until he was recently replaced by a younger family member. Many of the year-round staff have worked here for years, and summer help, especially the college students, tend to return season after season, as do some of the guests.

This is an excellent place to bring children. It is a hotel from the days when families fled to the breezy ocean beaches to escape the heat of inland summer and remained for a long time. They usually ate their meals where they stayed. You may still do it that way at the Chesterfield.

The menu always has choices of three or four entrées, including fresh seafood and at least three vegetables. The cooking is mostly Southern country as opposed to haute cuisine, tasty but not fancy.

The inn has thirty-two rooms. An adjacent motel with all the privileges of the inn has twenty-six rooms. All rooms have private bath, television, and telephone. Some motel rooms have wheelchair access.

SERENDIPITY
401 71st Street North
Myrtle Beach, SC 29577
(803) 449–5268
Rates: $48 to $85 including continental breakfast.
Closed December, January, and February.

Serendipity looks like a kind of Latin American mission hostelry, with its balcony arches and pink exterior. Each of the twelve rooms is decorated in a different theme mostly with antiques.

Cos and Ellen Ficarra, the innkeepers, say that they try to offer all the services you expect in a resort lodging—heated pool, Jacuzzi, shuffleboard—and still maintain the kind of atmosphere you enjoy at a bed and breakfast inn.

When continental breakfast is served in the dining area of the lobby, people tend to linger over second and third cups of coffee, chatting from table to table and swapping travel stories with Cos and Ellen. Occasionally Ellen gets so involved in a conversation that she forgets a batch of biscuits until Cos asks her if something's burning. It never seems to matter when that happens because the supply of biscuits and other breads is steady. Serendipity is right for travelers who like personal attention and an alternative to the sameness of standard motels and hotels.

All the rooms have private bath, refrigerators, and television.

SEA ISLAND
6000 North Ocean Boulevard
Myrtle Beach, SC 29577
800–548–0767
Rates: $32 to $105, breakfast and dinner optional.
Open year-round.

Sea Island is a modern luxury inn on the oceanfront differing from many of the big hotels in that it is located away from the heart of the vacation area in a residential section of Myrtle Beach. If this inn seems a little friendlier, a little better run than some, perhaps it is because it is managed by Matthew Brittain, son of Clay Brittain, who as long-time manager of the Chesterfield Inn provided a fine example of the personal approach to innkeeping. People who work at Sea Island say it is special.

All the rooms are oceanfront. Each has a private balcony overlooking the beach. The dining room also fronts on the ocean and serves breakfast and dinner.

There are two swimming pools, one of them heated, as well as wading pools, 110 rooms, and 46 efficiency apartments.

Dining

The traveler who can't find something appealing in Myrtle Beach and environs just plain doesn't like food. From haute cusine seafood to fast-food belly bombs, it's all here. Many restaurants are concentrated in Restaurant Row, a stretch along US 17 from Myrtle Beach North to Windy Hill devoted almost entirely to restaurants. You probably couldn't find a really bad meal among them. The restaurants listed here are well established and professionally run.

SLUG'S RIB OF MYRTLE BEACH

On Restaurant Row, 9713 US 17
Myrtle Beach
(803) 449–6419
Open for dinner seven days a week. Closed Christmas and New Year's Day.
All spirits available.

An upscale restaurant specializing in beef (something of a rarity in seafood country), Slug's of Myrtle Beach is one of several restaurants in a successful, family-owned group in the Carolinas. Although prime rib is the specialty, seafood, veal, daily specials, and a salad bar are always available too. An outdoor lounge overlooks the Intracoastal Waterway. Service is professional but not formal.

GULLYFIELD RESTAURANT
> On Restaurant Row, US 17 North
> Myrtle Beach
> (803) 449–3111
> Open for dinner seven days a week. Closed from end of
> November to mid-February.
> All spirits available.

Gullyfield's is one of the long-established seafood restaurants, in operation since 1974. The lattice work, white table tops, and plants of the interior create a casual outdoor garden atmosphere. There's nothing casual about the food, however. Fresh grilled king mackeral, a local fish, appeals to many diners. Grilled mahi-mahi and lobster pie are popular specialties from farther away.

OUTRIGGER SEAFOOD
> 1434 US 17 South
> Crescent Beach section of North Myrtle Beach
> (803) 272–8032
> Open for dinner seven days a week. Closed from
> Thanksgiving to February.
> All spirits available.

Outrigger Seafood House is a more elaborate version of the popular Southern "fish camps" that serve a limited variety of fried and broiled seafood in simple, camplike surroundings. As the popularity of the place grew, owner Lattie Upchurch expanded the menu to include more variety than you find in a standard fish camp. Instead of building additional restaurants to handle the increasing business, a common practice at Myrtle Beach, Upchurch simply kept adding rooms onto the existing restaurant. The result is a maze that twists and turns and rambles through a series of eight rooms, all different. In one, pictures of famous golf holes on local courses are features. In another, murals of beach scenes and golf courses completely cover the walls, even turning the corners. Huge aquariums of goldfish, tropical fish, and saltwater fish dominate another room.

As for the menu, seafood leads. You can order such gourmet preparations as grouper béarnaise, shrimp, crab, and scallops en casserole, or simpler steamed, broiled, and fried dishes. Steaks, chicken, and spaghetti are also available. Soups are homemade. Some of the specialties are offered as "all you can eat feasts," but even orders without that label are served in gargantuan proportions.

People come here dressed in everything from shorts to Sunday best. A couple of young people's Sunday school groups may come in at the same time as a golf party and an anniversary celebration party. The place is big and busy, but it works, and it's so friendly you feel down-home. Practically everyone gets a greeting from Lattie Upchurch, who always asks if everything was okay. Everything almost always is.

RISTORANTE VILLA ROMANA
707 South Kings Highway
Myrtle Beach
(803) 448–4990
Open for dinner Monday through Saturday. Closed
Christmas and New Year's Day.
All spirits available.

The restaurant is decorated like a Roman villa. Dining tables are arranged among statues, columns, and a fountain with live plants. Ornate chandeliers provide lighting for the scene. The family that runs Villa Romana and the chefs who prepare the food call themselves "native Romans." They boast that their meals combine traditional Italian recipes with new trends. Soups, pasta, and bread are all made fresh daily. Veal is hand-cut every day. When it's offered, the lamb is pink, juicy, delicately touched with garlic, about as close to perfect as it's possible for food to get. Another excellent dish is the potato gnocchi served in veal spezzato. Don't eat here if you plan to stick to a weight-loss diet.

The restaurant usually has live music, which inspires old Mamma Lucia to dance from time to time as she circulates among the diners asking in her minimal English, "You enjoy? Is good?"

VILLA MARE

7819 Kings Highway in Northwood Plaza
Myrtle Beach
(803) 449–8654
Open for lunch and dinner Monday through Saturday, only dinner on Sunday. Open year-round.
Domestic and imported beer available.

Villa Mare is an unpretentious storefront restaurant where the menu runs from hoagies, pizza, and calzone to excellent homemade pastas and a few chicken and veal dishes. As one "real Italian" man expressed it when recommending the place, "They know how to cook Italian." And with no modesty at all, a waitress reported, "Everybody who comes here is impressed."

MARINA RAW BAR RESTAURANT AND DECK

US 17 North
North Myrtle Beach
(803) 249–3972
Open for lunch and dinner seven days a week. Open year-round.
All spirits available.

Originally this restaurant was in a modest marina where you could look out at everything from a houseboat to some pretty fancy yachts as you ate. The marina has been closed, and what you look at now is a couple of new restaurants nearby. But the dock, the water, and the ducks attracted by them remain, and the restaurant, which is popular with local people as well as travelers, thrives.

The menu offers mostly seafood, with a few charbroiled steaks and burgers for the infidels who would sit in the land of fish and eat cows. This is a good place to order an oyster roast or steamed clams. The boiled shrimp in the shell is always excellent, as is the fresh tuna when available. Whatever you order, the standard accompaniments are hushpuppies, cole slaw, and french fries. You can get baked potatoes at dinner.

The nicest place to eat is on the glassed-in deck overlooking the water. Sometimes the odor of disinfectant inside can be bothersome.

TOBY'S RESTAURANT AND RAW BAR
US 17
Little River
(803) 249–2624
Open for dinner seven days a week. Closed in December.
All spirits available.

The people here call the atmosphere "fine dining casual," which is to say the dress is casual, the dining area is attractive, and the food is upscale gourmet—for example, scallops and oysters wrapped in bacon, Maryland style crabcakes, and steak au poivre. Toby has been responsible for creating a number of restaurants in the area; at each, sauces, soups, and special preparations with his name have appeared as house specialties. Usually these are rich and tasty concoctions.

Day Trips

You'll find it impossible to tell, except by reading the signs, where Myrtle Beach ends and North Myrtle Beach or Surfside and Garden City (both to the south) begin. One area runs into the next in a string of offerings.

A short drive from this concentration of beach-based tourist activities through some lesser developed countryside will take you to a number of special places, any of which, depending on your personal interests, could well be worth a day of your time.

BROOKGREEN GARDENS

On the west side of US 17, 18 miles south of Myrtle Beach
at Murrells Inlet.
(803) 237–4218
Open every day but Christmas.
Admission $5 for adults, $2.00 for children 6–12. Rates
include many free programs and tours.

Brookgreen Gardens is big and well known among people
interested in both figurative statues and native flora and
fauna. Whether the gardens serve as setting for the statues or
the sculptures as adornments for the gardens probably depends on whether you're looking as an artist or a horticultur-
ist. There are more than 500 pieces of art in this outdoor
museum, but there are also more than 2,000 different kinds of
plants. In addition to daily programs and tours, Brookgreen
Gardens offers periodic seminars about growing native plants.
It is a good place to visit if you like to see how Southeastern
plants grow and what wildlife they attract. It's also interesting
to see what exotic plants have been introduced successfully.
As for the statuary, Brookgreen Gardens is said to have the
largest permanent collection of American figurative sculpture
in the world, and it is still growing. Created in all media, from
marble and bronze to aluminum, the statues are realistic
rather than abstract.

In the 1700s, long before it was a park for statuary and horticulture, the property was a rice and indigo plantation. The
broad avenue shaded by moss-draped live oaks evokes images
of the plantation. You get the notion that this is how a plantation *should* look. The plantation's old formal garden design
was incorporated into Brookgreen's larger design. The paths
are laid out in the shape of a butterfly. The gardens flower
most of the year, beginning with early spring azaleas, and con-
tinuing into September with the vivid oranges and reds of fall.

A wildlife park shelters birds, otter, foxes, deer, and other
indigenous animals as well as a life-sized sculpture, *Alligator*,
by David Turner. A nature trail meandering through an aviary
gives you glimpses not only of the birds but also of wild-
flowers and old, old trees. If you're willing to pick a spot to sit

and then be quiet for a while, you'll enjoy some rewarding glimpses of the animals, too. This isn't as difficult to manage as you might suppose in a public place. Perhaps because of the expanses of grass and trees, the place seems surprisingly quiet, even when other people are nearby. For more noisy activity, you'll enjoy the picnic facilities established in appealing grassy areas.

HUNTINGTON BEACH STATE PARK
3 miles south of Murrells Inlet on US 17.
(803) 237–4440
Open year-round.
Admission $3 per automobile, $15 for multipassenger vans and busses.

On the opposite side of US 17 from Brookgreen Gardens, Huntington Beach State Park has 2,500 acres where you'll find one of South Carolina's nicest unspoiled beaches, especially good for shelling. Much of the park's land is devoted to preserving the natural habitat, and the site is excellent for birding. Nature trails and programs are offered year-round. You can fish from a jetty, use one of the more than 120 campsites, and cross a boardwalk over the salt marsh. Also located on the grounds is Atalaya, known as "the castle," the studio and summer home of the American sculptor Anna Hyatt Huntington and her husband Archer Huntington, who founded Brookgreen Gardens.

MURRELLS INLET

This little community 6 miles south of Myrtle Beach on US 17 is for people who like to eat—really like to eat. The village, said to be named for a pirate who used to hang around, had a population of 210 in the early 1940s, according to the *WPA Guide to the Palmetto State*, and even today is permanent home to fewer than 3,000 people. The inlet has always been known for good fishing and crabbing, although today you're more likely to get your catch from one of the seafood restaurants by the water than to wade into the marsh for it. You'll find stands selling shrimp fresh from the boat. You can charter deep-sea fishing trips from here, too.

But to get back to the eating, the restaurants in Murrells Inlet are casual places known for their oyster roasts. An oyster roast is a huge kettle full of rock oysters (the kind that come in clumps), steamed just long enough to open the shells, served with lemon and butter and a roll of paper towels. As you eat the oysters, you toss the shells through a hole in the center of the table into a trash can underneath.

Fresh broiled and fried seafoods are always on the menu too. Sometimes you're offered a choice of portion sizes: small, medium, or large. Before you go ordering anything large, take a look at what's being served around you. Portions in South Carolina seafood houses usually would be more accurately labeled large, giant, and gargantuan. People who eat in these restaurants a lot don't just loosen their belts a notch or so; eventually they wear the belts under their bellies, and these bellies clearly reflect the ordering habits of the belt owners. Order for yourself accordingly.

GEORGETOWN

The third oldest city in South Carolina, located on US 17 about 35 miles south of Myrtle Beach, Georgetown boasts a lot of history for so small a community. The historic district, on the Sampit River, dates back to the 1700s. The entire district is listed on the National Register of Historic Places. As a steady source of income, tourism represents an important part of the district's revitalization.

Before the Revolutionary War the city's money came mainly from making and shipping indigo. Then rice became the main crop. By 1840 Georgetown county produced nearly half of the rice crop of the United States. Although industrialization has since replaced rice, Georgetown's deep harbor accommodates oceangoing ships and still functions as an important shipping port.

The little community has quite a few specialty and clothing shops, and three restaurants line Front Street by the river. Of these, River Room, 817 Front Street, is especially popular with business people and tourists at lunch time. The restaurant serves iced tea in wide-mouthed Ball jars, has a nice wine selection, and makes great seafood salads. Another of their notable specialties is homemade french fried onion rings. The caveat regarding belts and bellies mentioned in regard to Murrells Inlet restaurants applies here too.

For local history, The Rice Museum (803–546–7423), at the corner of Front Street and Screven Street, has exhibits and information about Georgetown's origins and development. The Georgetown Chamber of Commerce (803–546–8436), 600 Front Street, offers tapes and brochures for self-guided tours.

Private tour companies, all of whose telephone numbers are available from the Georgetown Chamber of Commerce, offer a variety of possibilities.

Probably the most comprehensive of the companies is Capt. Sandy's Tours, an energetic operation run by Sandy Vermont, a South Carolina storyteller who believes that an area's history, culture, and stories explain each other. Operating from this assumption, Capt. Sandy's now runs tram tours of the historic district plus three different boat tours: waterway plantation tours, shell collecting tours, and ghost story tours. Sandy says the ghost story tours start at dark and star an old storyteller whose tales "make you think about yourself."

By the time you are reading this guide, Sandy expects to have added an outdoor storytelling drama featuring Miss Effie as the storyteller, with actors who pantomime the action, a historian who explains it, and a musical score to puncutate it. Eventually, Sandy promises, he'll add an outdoor program of plantation spirituals based on the songs of the old rice culture, which originally were sung by dock workers and field hands.

Capt. Sandy's offerings are available year-round, weather permitting. If you show up with a bus load of people, he can provide a "step-on guide" to ride along, direct the driver, and explain the sights. For reservations and current details about this changing and growing operation, phone Capt. Sandy at (803) 527–4106.

If you'd like more time in Georgetown, you might enjoy staying at the Shaw House, 8 Cypress Court (zip code 29440,

phone 803–546–9663), which is open year-round. This little
bed and breakfast inn is run by Mary Shaw, who is becoming
something of a celebrity among travelers for her easy hospitality. The house is furnished with antiques, which Mary talks
about not in terms of their value or historic significance but in
relationship to her family. She's full of stories about how she
and her husband found or inherited various pieces and what
they did to make them usable.

Mary's brand of hospitality includes a whopping big breakfast with a pot of coffee for each guest, and snacks and drinks
in the evening. The house sits on a bluff overlooking the salt
marsh, and Mary will make sure you don't miss the view. Picture windows near the breakfast table make this a splendid
place for bird-watching.

The inn has three rooms with private bath. Telephone and
television are available by arrangement. Call the number
above for rates.

CONWAY

From US 17 at Myrtle Beach pick up US 501 North and follow it to Conway. Take Business 501 to get into town. Conway is a little inland town you pass almost without noticing,
unless you're looking for it, on your way to Myrtle Beach. It's
worth stopping for.

Driving up and down the streets of the residential areas you
discover the quintessential old Southern town with a surprising number of fine old homes, many built by shipbuilders.
Spanish moss drapes ancient live oaks. These trees are so re-
vered that paved streets and sidewalks have been curved
around them to keep them from having to be cut down.

For a driving tour to see some of the local historical buildings, you can pick up a map at the Conway Chamber of Commerce, 203 Main Street (803–248–2273); it is open Monday
through Saturday 9:00 A.M. to 5:00 P.M.

A couple of blocks away from the Chamber of Commerce is
the Horry County Museum, 438 Main Street (803–248–1282
or 626–6480). It is open Monday through Saturday 10:00

A.M. to 5:00 P.M., and admission is free. The museum features exhibits emphasizing how Horry County residents adapted to various local environmental conditions from prehistoric times to the present to survive. One of the most unusual exhibits is a thirty-five-foot-long mural-like map of the Waccamaw River, showing the locations and telling the stories of the old landings and ferries. The staff created the map by projecting geological maps onto the wall and tracing them. "The hardest part was getting the scales to match," said museum director William Keeling. In an exhibit on woodworking you'll find a foot-driven lathe built in 1930 by a Conway man who had no electricity. The museum rotates work by local artists and crafters every month. Some of it is for sale.

Conway is the county seat of Horry County. This inspired the name of a delightful pioneering restaurant in town, in an old building that used to be a plant store. It is the County Seat Cafe, at 111 Third Avenue (803–248–3733). The restaurant is open for lunch Tuesday through Friday 11:30 A.M. to 2:00 P.M., dinner Tuesday through Saturday 5:30 P.M. to 9:00 P.M. There's a Saturday mid-morning gourmet breakfast/brunch from 10:00 A.M. to 1:00 P.M. The food here differs dramatically from typical small-town Southern cooking. At lunch, specialties include a Thai salad and a huge stuffed baked potato. For dinner the most popular choice is pork tenderloin schnitzel, with Roger's creamy seafood pasta (based on a champagne-mushroom sauce) running it a close second. All spirits are available, including good, moderately priced varietal wines.

Midlands

The South Carolina State Museum
photo by Dan Smith

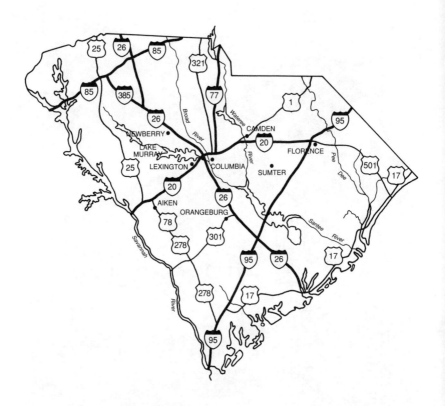

COLUMBIA

Columbia presents the visitor with several different faces. The city has been the capital of South Carolina since 1786 and as such has a rich history which long-time Columbians commemorate passionately. If you meet these people over dinner, expect to hear before you get to dessert how Sherman burned the city but spared the college (now the University of South Carolina) because Union troops were hospitalized there. Despite the fires, the city has some excellent restored homes open for touring which originally belonged to important South Carolina families.

At the same time, energetic, enterprising business people and artisans are expanding Columbia's cultural and professional horizons with such initiatives as the Congaree Vista Redevelopment Program. Centered in the area between Gervais Street and Lady Street, west of Assembly, the Congaree Vista covers 900 acres along the Congaree riverfront. Here you will find growing numbers of antiques shops, artists' studios and galleries, restaurants, and architects' offices. The Congaree Vista Guild sponsors Vista Lights each November to celebrate the renaissance of the area. During this time shops extend their hours until 9:00 P.M., the streets are candlelit, and special performing arts programs from theater to street music are scheduled. During the rest of the year the Vista artists independently schedule special activities at their galleries, especially in April and September. If you have a special interest in the arts and would like to see more about the Vista activities, phone (803) 256–1873 for current details.

The Five Points area, near the university, reflects the tastes and traditions of academia and also a younger, trendy population with a variety of restaurants, a gourmet shop, an art gallery, and other stores offering a range of goods from clothing to antiques.

Of course, the University of South Carolina, established in 1805 with two professors and nine students, also exerts a significant influence on the area. When it's empty, the campus quadrangle, known as the Horseshoe, with its composition of brick walks and buildings patterned after English universities, calls to mind the gracious, slower times of the old South. But when students and faculty are out rushing from one class to another, chattering about grades and football (though probably in reverse order), you become aware of the university as a source of energy in the community.

Another influence in Columbia's makeup is the Fort Jackson U.S. Army training base, which has been there since 1917 and continues to be an important army base today. Uniformed men and women are a highly visible presence in the city. A museum at 4442 Jackson Boulevard details the history of training soldiers and displays military equipment. Phone (803) 751–7419 for full details.

The old and the new are coming together in Columbia's residential areas, too. Although Columbia has a full share of newish housing developments, usually with birds or trees or bodies of water in their names, an outstanding renovation movement thrives in established neighborhoods such as the Shandon area. A drive up Blossom Street is a good way to get into that neighborhood.

Activities and Attractions

To get a quick course in Columbia's history and architecture, try touring the historic homes (listed below) held and managed by the Richland County Historic Preservation Commission (803–252–1770).

All homes are open year-round Tuesday through Saturday 10:15 A.M. to 3:15 P.M., Sunday 1:15 P.M. to 4:15 P.M. Closed mid-December through January 2 and major holidays.

Admission $3 for adults, $1.50 for students 6–21.

ROBERT MILLS HISTORIC HOUSE AND PARK
1616 Blanding Street

The name of the house derives from its designer, who also designed the Washington Monument. The house was intended as the home of a well-to-do merchant who died before it was finished. Instead it housed a series of religious organizations. It was nearly torn down in 1961, but preservationists saved it. They restored it according to information found in Mills's old manuscripts and in Historic American Building Survey documents in Washington, D.C. This is an elegant house, with matching drawing rooms, marble mantelpieces, and silver doorknobs. It is furnished with Regency furniture. The property includes four acres of formal landscaping.

HAMPTON-PRESTON MANSION AND GARDEN (CIRCA 1818–1835)
1615 Blanding Street

An interesting feature of this property, in addition to its having been owned by General Wade Hampton and by the Prestons, is the ongoing restoration of the gardens and fountains based on old horticultural records. Inside, most of the furnishings are those of the Hampton families. The Hampton sisters, who served as hostesses for their father, Wade Hampton II, took entertaining very seriously, in spite of hard times. The label on an exhibit entitled "The Legend of the Tablecloth" tells the story and gives extraordinary insight into the values and mentality of the times in Columbia:

> The War Between the States brought deprivation to everyone in Columbia. However, even among the ruins people made an effort to maintain a polite society. For example, the Hampton sisters discovered that the rector of Trinity Episcopal Church, the Reverend Peter Shand, was dining off a bare table. They presented him with the tablecloth shown here, which was made from a bolt of linen ordered by Wade Hampton II from Ireland for

Millwood Plantation. The state symbol, a palmetto tree, is woven into the border.

Never again did the reverend have to entertain at dinner from a bare table.

Many old-time Columbians are just as concerned today about propriety.

WOODROW WILSON BOYHOOD HOME (CIRCA 1872)
1705 Hampton Street

Woodrow Wilson, son of a Presbyterian minister, spent three of his teenage years in this house in the late 1800s. It's considered a good example of a minister's Victorian home and contains some furnishings and smaller items which belonged to the Wilsons.

MANN-SIMONS COTTAGE (CIRCA 1850)
1403 Richland Street

This is the only historic house museum in Columbia to have belonged to an antebellum black family, and even today it is rare in being devoted to the black history of the area. Celia Mann, a slave in Charleston, bought her freedom, walked to Columbia, and set up a family home here in 1850. It belonged to people of her family until the Columbia Housing Authority bought it in 1970. The museum contains family items and has a gallery and gift shop specializing in work by black artists.

SOUTH CAROLINA STATE MUSEUM
301 Gervais Street
(803) 737-4921
Open Monday through Saturday 10:00 A.M. to 5:00 P.M., Sunday 1:00 P.M. to 5:00 P.M.
Admission $3 for adults; $2.00 for senior citizens, military, and college students with I.D.; $1.25 for children 6–17, free for children under 6.

This is the largest museum in the state and one of the largest in the South. Work by South Carolina artists or having a South

Carolina theme occupies the first floor. The second floor contains exhibits about natural history, the third science and technology. If you are traveling with children, don't miss the science gallery. Youngsters can light up a laser beam, talk into the whisper dish and hear their voices across the room, and handle such marvels as the fossilized teeth of an extinct American mastadon. Cultural exhibits take up the fourth floor.

Equally absorbing for all ages, the transportation exhibit features a 1904 open Oldsmobile that looks more like a buggy than an automobile. It is steered with a tiller handle rather than a wheel. Also in the exhibit, emphasizing how transportation has changed in less than a hundred years, you'll see a space suit worn by General Charles M. Duke, Jr., one of several astronauts from South Carolina.

The museum building itself holds interest. It was the world's first totally electric textile mill. The Mount Vernon Mills made cotton duck from 1894 until 1981. It reopened as a museum in 1988, which makes it relatively young (in museum terms) to have built such a comprehensive collection.

COLUMBIA MUSEUM OF ART
1112 Bull Street
(803) 799–2810
Open Tuesday through Friday 10:00 A.M. to 5:00 P.M.,
Saturday and Sunday 12:30 P.M. to 5:00 P.M. Closed holidays.
Admission free.

Notable for its changing exhibits in contemporary and traditional art, photography, and the decorative arts, the museum also has the Samuel H. Kress Collection. It's known as one of the better permanent collections of Baroque and Renaissance art in the Southeast. Other artists represented include Monet, Matisse, Renoir, Jasper Johns, and such regional artists as Elizabeth O'Neill Verner.

Saturday and Sunday afternoons the Gibbes Planetarium presents multimedia programs including the show "Carolina Skies," about the stars, planets, and constellations that you can see at night with the naked eye. Call ahead to check on exact time for specific shows.

CONFEDERATE RELIC ROOM AND MUSEUM
    920 Sumter Street
    (803) 734–9813
    Open Monday through Friday 8:30 A.M. to 5:00 P.M.
    Admission free.

Although this is a smaller museum, visiting it is a poignant experience. The museum's relic collection covers everything from the Colonial period to recent space shots, but the Civil War items speak most eloquently of real people involved in real struggle. You see it, for instance, in two Confederate uniforms. The first, from early in the war, was professionally tailored and looks like the uniforms one sees in famous paintings of the Confederate Army. The other was homemade near the end of the war from homespun fabric dyed with roots and acorns. A lady's dress made during Reconstruction from drapery fabric and a worn beaded purse call to mind the scene in *Gone with the Wind* in which Scarlet wore a dress improvised from dining room curtains.

STATE HOUSE
    Main Street at Gervais
    (803) 734–2430
    Open Monday through Friday 9:00 A.M. to 4:00 P.M. Tours conducted on the half-hour.
    Admission free.

This Classical blue granite structure, largely completed by 1855, survived shelling in 1865 by Sherman's troops, situated across the Congaree River. Today it bears six bronze stars on its west wall to mark the spots that were hit. The State House dome was added in 1900. Among the interesting architectural and structural features inside are marble floors, balconies with brass railings, and mahogany woodwork. The lawns, with their garden spots and monuments, are a popular place to walk or to sit on a bench and relax.

McKissick Museum

On the Horseshoe of USC campus
(803) 777–7251
Open Monday through Friday 9:00 A.M. to 5:00 P.M.,
Saturday 10:00 A.M. to 5:00 P.M., Sunday 1:00 P.M. to 5:00 P.M.
Admission free.

Exhibits here change frequently. They emphasize art, science, regional history, and folk art. Depending on when you visit, you may see quilts and textiles, student art, Southeastern art, pottery, photography, or articles related to African American culture. The Smith geology area features a fine display of regional minerals.

The museum building housed the university's library before the Thomas Cooper Library was built. The walk to and around McKissick takes you through one of the loveliest parts of the campus.

Riverbanks Zoological Park

Greystone Boulevard and I–26
(803) 779–8730 (for hours); (803) 779–8717 (other information)
Open daily 9:00 A.M. to 4:00 P.M.
Admission $3.75 for adults; $3.00 for children 13–18;
$1.75 for children 3–12; $2.50 for senior citizens over 62.

Columbians are proud of their zoo's rating as one of the nation's top ten. Riverbanks now has about 2,000 animals kept in natural settings without cages, ranging from sea lions to penguins. The focus of the zoo, however, is its aquarium-reptile complex, which houses 1,000 reptiles, amphibians, and fish from around the world. This indoor display, consisting of five galleries and shaped like a doughnut, represents different areas of the world. You move first into the South Carolina gallery of indigenous snakes, fish, and other reptiles, then into a desert gallery, and so on. The tropical habitat where you find such creatures as crocodiles is hot and humid, like a greenhouse. Open-topped glass barriers separate the animals from the people.

One of the most popular outdoor features is the recently re-vamped African Plains exhibits, featuring black rhinos (an en-dangered species), zebras, a herd of giraffes, and a few ostriches.

CONGAREE SWAMP NATIONAL MONUMENT
Superintendent's address: 200 Caroline Sims Road
Hopkins, SC 29061
(803) 776–4396
Open daily 8:30 A.M. to 5:00 P.M. except Christmas.
Admission free.

Ordinarily a swamp probably wouldn't make it into a guide book, but Congaree Swamp is interesting to know about even if you decide not to go there. The swamp is created by periodic flooding of the Congaree River. The elevation of the flood-plain varies from a hundred feet above sea level to eighty feet. When the waters come flooding in, animals survive either by swimming to high points or waiting up in trees or even on floating logs for the water to recede.

For people, the swamp has twenty miles of hiking trails and two boardwalks, each about three-fourths of a mile long. The high boardwalk runs from three to seven feet above the ground, with railings to keep you up there. The lower board-walk, close to the ground, requires you to keep your own bal-ance. Both boardwalks lead to two lakes full of large-mouth bass, bream, and crappie. To fish, you hike in or ride a bike in on the service road to a spot near the fishing access.

In addition to hiking and fishing, the swamp is a wonderful place to study natural history. Floodplains are known for their fertility, which is due largely to rich soil that comes in with the floodwater. In a healthy swamp, the topography documents a distinct life cycle that begins when a big tree falls, letting in light that encourages new plants to grow. The tree's roots heave out of the earth, and the soil falls off the roots, creating a mound around the hole in which the tree had been growing. The accumulated result of this phenomenon is called pit-and-mound topography.

Foresters classify four kinds of swamp growth: high canopy, second canopy, understory or forest floor, and emergent trees.

These latter rise above the canopy into full light but receive less humidity, which means that they are different from the trees thriving in the canopy layers. In the Congaree there are sweet gums throughout; sycamores and tupelos at the lowest levels; and hollies, cherrybark oaks, and loblolly pines at the higher levels. You'll find loblollies growing as high as 145 feet, with poison ivy climbing around them almost as high. (Other hazards include wasps in fall and summer.) A wealth of wildlife accompanies the diversity of flora.

You can explore the park with or without guides, on foot or by canoe. It's a good idea to call before you visit to arrange the outing most suited to your skills and interests.

To get to Congaree Swamp, take Bluff Road (SC 48) east for 10.7 miles past the University of South Carolina Stadium. On your right you will see a sign saying "Congaree Swamp National Monument." Bear right onto Old Bluff Road. Go 4.6 miles to another swamp sign. Turn right and go for one mile to the Ranger Station, where you must register your vehicle.

Lodging

Driving around the outskirts of Columbia, you get the impression of a motel in every block. In addition to the standard chains you find many newer motels with signs advertising low prices. Generally, any of those that look tidy and well kept from the outside are the same inside. They are not bad bargains.

For more unusual accommodations, try the following.

CLAUSSEN'S INN
    2003 Greene Street
    (803) 765–0440; outside South Carolina (800) 622–3382
    Rates: $85 to $100

The building used to be Claussen's Bakery. It still looks like a bakery from outside. Inside, the space has been done over to create an open, skylit lobby with lots of potted plants, a fountain, and bright, soft couches and chairs.

The twenty-nine rooms, most of which have twenty-foot-high ceilings, are done with antique reproductions and such subtleties as armoires to hide the television sets. For a real splurge, the loft suites are spectacular, with separate sitting areas, full-length windows, and hardwood floors.

All rooms have private bath, television, and telephone; some have wheelchair access.

GOVERNOR'S HOUSE HOTEL
   1301 Main Street
   (803) 779–7790 or (800) 325–2525
   Rates: $39 to $57

The hotel is just a block from the capitol. It's a pleasant five-floor building built in 1962, not old by the standards of preservationists, but still old enough not to have that over-shiny gloss that makes so many hotels seem alike. The Governor's House Hotel is now a Days Inn, but that hasn't spoiled it. Days Inn lodgings are locally owned, and each maintains its individual character, unlike those franchises which specify everything from the color of the drapes to the protocol at the front desk.

The lobby makes the point. It is a quaint, warm room with marble, varnished oak, brass, and an olive carpet. In keeping with this, there is (ah, miracle!) no computer. Records and reservations and billing are all managed by hand, by real people with pencils and pens and file cards.

The guest rooms are nicely furnished with 18-century reproductions.

The hotel has nearly 100 rooms. All rooms have telephones and television; some have refrigerators. The hotel has a pool.

Continental breakfast is included in rates.

TOWN HOUSE
   1615 Gervais Street
   (803) 771–8711 or (800) 277–8711
   Rates: $51 to $70

Recently remodeled, the Town House has long been a preferred place in Columbia to bunk visiting artists and government dignitaries. It is close to the capitol and downtown Columbia. The tower section of the hotel is six stories high; a lower courtyard section appeals to people who like to park outside their rooms. The guest rooms are variously furnished in standard modern style with coordinated bedding, carpet, and drapes. The hotel has a pool, restaurant, and lounge. It is the meeting spot for a shag club. Shag is the state dance of South Carolina, described by one shagger as "kind of like jitterbugging barefoot in the sand." Some enthusiasts carry it to forms as elaborate as Western swing, but you can master the basic step in a short time. If you want to be sure to get in a night of shagging, ask about current schedules when you make your reservations.

The hotel has 147 rooms, all with private bath, television, and telephone.

Dining

It wasn't so long ago in Columbia that your food choices were between Southern cooking and Southern cooking, but as Columbia's population has grown, so has the diversity of its restaurants. Most of those listed here are in some way unique in Columbia. Some are especially popular with the long-time area residents, while others enjoy special favor among the "transplants" as well as with people who've been around for a while.

A. J.'s

> 2864 Devine Street
> (803) 254–0699
> Open for lunch and dinner Monday through Saturday,
> Sunday brunch.
> All spirits available.

A. J.'s has been around for a long time. It's a testimony to the food and the atmosphere (a kind of uptown business people's place) that people come here now as much as in the days when diners had fewer choices. The service is casual but efficient. The homemade soups are especially worth ordering. At lunch the most popular choices include salads, pasta, grilled meats, and fresh fish. For dinner the offerings include shrimp fettuccini, prime rib, crabcakes, and grilled fish.

BASIL POT
928 Main Street
(803) 799–0928
Open Monday through Friday 8:00 A.M.-2:30 P.M. and 6:00 P.M.-9:30 P.M., Saturday 6:00 P.M.-9:30 P.M., Sunday 9:00 A.M.-2:30 P.M. Breakfast served until 11:00 A.M. Monday through Friday and all day Sunday.
Wine and beer available.

The Basil Pot is located on the part of Main Street that resumes behind the State House, not the part that runs through the center of downtown. Once strictly vegetarian, several years ago the restaurant added chicken, turkey, shrimp, tuna, and other fish to its menu. Many people do come here, though, for the vegetarian entrées and combination plates, the latter of which include rice, some kind of beans, and steamed vegetables. These change daily, as do all the specials. The homemade muffins and breads are good; so are the unusual salad dressings. Exhibits by local artists adorn the walls. No smoking is allowed.

CAMON JAPANESE
1332 Assembly Street
(803) 254–5400
Open for lunch and dinner Monday through Friday, dinner only Saturday. Closed Sunday. Reservations available.
Beer and wine available.

This small, authentic Japanese restaurant has a nice sushi bar for those who dare. You can order sampler trays of sashimi, too. Other food, such as sukiyaki, is cooked at your table. Or you can order feathery light tempura dishes. Japanese beer or sake complements the foods. With a restaurant as small and intimate as this one, calling ahead for reservations is essential to avoid disappointment.

COLUMBIA'S
1201 Main Street
(803) 799–3071
Open Monday through Friday 11:30 A.M. to midnight, Saturday 5:00 P.M. to midnight.
All spirits available.

Columbia's is in the AT&T building, at the corner of Main and Gervais. Looking out its expansive front windows, you can see part of the State House lawn. The restaurant is a study in art deco, all sleek surfaces and lots of pink, gray, and black. The menu includes fresh fish, pork, and steak dishes, and the chef changes specials daily. One of the best things about Columbia's, though, for all its elegance, is that you can get just an appetizer or small meal at any time, with no frowns from the friendly servers. Dinner reservations recommended.

ELITE EPICUREAN
1736 Main Street
(803) 765–2325
Open Monday through Saturday 6:00 A.M. to 11 P.M. Closed Sunday and holidays.
All spirits available.

Try this place if you want to be sure of seeing some of the people who have been in town for years and years. The restaurant is right across the street from City Hall. It's popular for lunch with such specials as moussaka and fish fillets, but the really good time is dinner. Then you can order some lavish seafood preparations. The baby squid stuffed with shrimp cooked in wine sauce is delightful. Vegetables don't get a lot of attention here; a house salad is about it, except for potatoes. The Epicurean potato is creamy, seasoned mashed potato on the inside with a crispy fried shell on the outside.

GOURMET SHOP

> 724 Saluda
> (803) 799–3705
> Open daily 9:00 A.M. to 3:45; open to 4:45 Saturday and Sunday.
> Beer and wine available.

The Gourmet Shop started out as a wine and cheese shop more than a decade ago in a small space near its current location. As the shop's owner identified and educated a growing market for more exotic foods and kitchen equipment, the place grew steadily, ultimately expanding to add the café. It serves an assortment of sandwiches, salads, and desserts using many of the same ingredients you can buy in the shop. The croissant sandwiches, made on fresh-daily croissants, are tremendously popular. On nice days you can sit at an outside table and watch shoppers walking along the street. If you eat indoors, the aromas of fresh coffee, herbs, and spices whet your appetite before you've even decided what you want.

HENNESSY'S

> 1649 Main Street
> (803) 799–8280
> Open for lunch Monday through Friday, dinner Monday through Saturday.
> All spirits available.

People often choose Hennessy's for dinner when they want to celebrate a special occasion. Housed in an old building that was once a hardware store, it has a relaxed but slightly formal atmosphere and decor, with linens on the table, fancy folded napkins, and work by local artists on the walls. The menu features steaks, veal, lamb, chicken, and seafood. The house specialty is crabcakes. At lunch you can order from a variety of daily specials, salads, and sandwiches.

IMMACULATE CONSUMPTION
    933 Main Street
    (803) 799–9053
    Opens at 11:00 A.M. Closes at 4:00 P.M. Monday and
    Tuesday, 9:00 P.M. Wednesday and Thursday, 11:00 P.M.
    Friday and Saturday.
    Beer and wine available.

    This is a lighthearted place specializing in tasty low-
fat food. The atmosphere is café-like, with old wood floors,
a decor of bright India blue and pink zigzags on the walls,
and puppets for ornamentation. One of the owners said,
"We have some real peculiar art work." The tables are
simple wood, some of them made by the owners from
doors.
    The food is excellent. They make their own soup and prac-
tically everything else. The chicken salad, made without may-
onnaise, has apples and spices to give it piquancy. The turkey
sandwich includes sliced green apples. The tuna salad has a
low-fat dill dressing.
    In keeping with the restaurant's name, after your meal you
recycle your own paper, cans, and bottles in labeled bins out
front.

INDIA PAVILION
    2011 Devine Street
    (803) 252–4355
    Open for lunch 11:30 A.M. to 3:00 P.M. Monday through
    Saturday, dinner 5:00 P.M. to 10:30 P.M. Monday through
    Sunday.
    Wine and beer available.

    This restaurant at Five Points specializes in Northern Indian
food—curries, tandoori chicken, vegetarian specialties, and
plenty of beef, lamb, and fish. Smoky-tasting Indian beer complements the spicy food.

MAURICE BESSINGER'S PIGGIE PARK
1600 Charleston Highway
West Columbia
(803) 796–0220
Open every day 10:00 A.M. to 11:00 P.M.

What you get at Maurice's Piggie Park isn't just a meal, it's an experience. It's a low, rambling place dominated by the piggie sign and by the aroma of Maurice's mustard-based barbeque sauce. The sauce has become so popular you can buy it by the bottle in retail stores. Running barbeque a close second in popularity is "hash," a ground pork concoction served over rice. You can order just a single sandwich, of course, but most often you see plates heaped with barbeque *and* hash and maybe fries, all to be washed down with sweetened ice tea, simply called "sweet tea."

MOTOR SUPPLY CO. BISTRO
920 Gervais Street
(803) 256–6687
Open for lunch Tuesday through Saturday 11:30 A.M. to 2:30 P.M., dinner 5:30 P.M. to 11:00 P.M., Sunday brunch 11:00 A.M. to 3:00 P.M., Sunday (Thai night) dinner 5:00 P.M. to 11:00 P.M.
All spirits available.

This place *was* an auto parts company thirty years ago. The people who turned it into a restaurant early in the Congaree Vista renaissance were going to call it the Vista Café, but they found the old sign in the basement and changed their minds. And that's the sign that marks the restaurant, which is acclaimed by food writers on several counts: a small menu that really does change daily for both lunch and dinner; good, fresh food at reasonable prices; and an atmosphere that's different and inviting. You can walk in the sculpture garden out back any time, and in good weather you can sit out there if you're lucky enough to get one of the few tables.

Banquet facilities are available, in case you're in town to put on a wedding. Reservations are needed for parties of eight or more.

ORIENTAL GARDEN
> 1710 Main Street
> (803) 765–9393
> Open for lunch and dinner Monday through Saturday.
> Beer and wine available.

At the Oriental Garden (across from the courthouse) exceptionally nice people serve exceptionally good Korean and Chinese food in an unpretentious setting. What's more, they'll explain every dish on the menu to you if you want to be sure of what you're getting before you order.

One of the most popular items on the menu is marinated beef served with lettuce leaves and hot sauce, sang-choo backbdan. A stir-fried mixture of vegetables and beef appeals to many diners, too. Side dishes of kimchi, pickled turnip and cabbage, set off all the flavors. Or order a big bowl of sum sun jum bong, a noodle soup that can be so spicy it brings tears to your eyes.

PARTHENON
> 734 Hardin Street
> 11:00 A.M. to 10:00 P.M.
> (803) 799–7754
> Beer and wine available.

What a find, a Greek restaurant run by Greeks, serving authentic food almost the same as you'd find in Greece. You step into the restaurant from the street and enter another world. Latticework separates the entry from the rest of the restaurant, which is dimly lit and cool. Greek music plays continuously. If you're not hungry when you enter, you will be soon. As servers carry food to the booths and tables you smell tantalizing hints of olive oil, tomato sauce, and rich cheeses. You can order such standard favorites as moussaka and baklava, but the Greek pizza is good too. The menu includes varied salads and an eggplant Parmesan sandwich that may be the most popular lunch item served.

RICHARD'S
936 Gervais Street
(803) 799–3071
Open for lunch Monday through Friday 11:30 A.M. to 2:30 P.M.; dinner Monday through Thursday 6:00 P.M. to 10:00 P.M., Friday and Saturday 6:00 P.M. to 11:00 P.M. Closed Sunday.
All spirits available.

Situated in a good old building in the Congaree Vista, this restaurant prides itself on "fine Southern cuisine," which is an understatement. It also has an elegant but not overwhelming atmosphere and attentive but unobtrusive service. On Saturday nights live entertainment accompanies dinner. Dinner reservations are recommended.

RESTAURANT AT CINNAMON HILL
808 S. Lake Drive
Just off I-20 on Highway 6
Lexington
(803) 957–8297
Open for lunch and dinner Tuesday through Saturday.
Reservations recommended.
All spirits available.

Because Lexington is close enough to seem like part of Columbia, many Columbians eat here regularly. An old Victorian building with charming nooks and crannies houses the restaurant. The menu includes assorted pasta dishes and fresh seafood as well as lamb, beef, and chicken.

YESTERDAY'S RESTAURANT AND TAVERN
    2030 Devine Street
    (803) 799–0196
    Open Sunday through Tuesday 11:30 A.M. to 1:00 A.M.,
    Wednesday through Saturday 11:30 A.M. to 2:00 A.M.
    All spirits available.

The food is American country style: prime rib, broiled chicken with gravy, Confederate fried steak with gravy. Also available are the more standard burgers, salads, etc.

Because of its location in the Five Points part of the city near the university, the capitol, and a lot of businesses, the atmosphere is college-town tavern, attracting students, faculty, local business folk, and some of those state employees responsible for running South Carolina.

An entertaining part of the atmosphere is the ample number of university pennants, mugs, and souvenir memorabilia honoring not the Gamecocks of the University of South Carolina but the Penn State Nittany Lions, of which one of the owners is a loyal fan. Roar, Lions, Roar!

Day Trips

Columbia makes an excellent central starting point for exploring midlands towns in every direction. In some cases you might choose to spend a night in one of them. Other times you can easily return to Columbia, with its wide range of services, rest up, and start out again the next day in another direction.

Lexington

This friendly community, growing but still somewhat rural in feeling and in fact, is 18 to 20 miles west of Columbia, depending on whether you take US 378, US 1, or US 126/I–20. Meeting as they do at the Lake Murray Dam, Lexington and Columbia seem so much of a piece that people sometimes fail to treat them separately. However, citizens' bumper stickers assert Lexington's independence from Columbia. As you explore the area, take time to stop at the Lexington County Museum Complex, where history gets a down-to-earth treatment. It is located at the corner of Fox Street and US 378 (Columbia Avenue) in downtown Lexington and is open from 10:00 A.M. to 4:00 P.M. Tuesday through Saturday and from 1:00 P.M. to 4:00 P.M. Sunday except on major holidays. Admission is $1.00 for adults, $.50 for children under 12. The museum's phone number is (803) 359–8369.

If you're interested in history as more than a collection of dates and think a museum should be more than a display of artifacts, this is the place to visit. Here you learn how a middle-class South Carolina farming family lived in the 1800s.

The complex comprises a furnished ten-room farmhouse built about 1830 and its outbuildings: kitchen, work house, dairy sheds, privy, and loom room.

The rooms are furnished as they would have been in the 1840s with country furniture made in the South Carolina midlands before 1865. The tables, chairs, corner cupboards, beds, and other pieces are made of pine, walnut, cherry, and sweet gum. Horace Harmon, director of the museum, says the exhibit is more important as a whole than are any of the individual items. "We don't show you fine rosewood and mahogany pieces and tell you what well-to-do person donated them. Instead, we're showing a middle-class lifestyle," he said. "You can see how people ate and slept, how they made feather beds, and what they used as coverlets."

Thirty people lived in the house, fifteen family members and fifteen slaves. Guided tours interpret the exhibits, explaining how the family would have used the items displayed.

The loom room is a popular stop on the tour because it contains a good collection of spinning and weaving equipment. Demonstrations of the tools here are available by appointment.

The most popular exhibit is the collection of quilts, the third largest in the state. All the quilts in this collection are from the local area.

The tour takes at least an hour, depending on how many questions you have. The exhibits also include collections of farm tools, but these are not emphasized, Harmon says, because by the time most people have seen everything else, they're too tired to poke around any more.

For food in Lexington, the old-timers favor Hite's, the intersection of US 378 and Main Street (803–359–2589). Country cooking is the specialty here, with a weekday buffet for lunch and dinner. On Friday and Saturday nights there's a seafood buffet and a country buffet—something for everybody. Hite's is open Tuesday 6:30 A.M. to 2:00 P.M., Wednesday through Saturday 6:30 A.M. to 9:00 P.M., and Sunday 11:30 A.M. to 2:00. It's closed on Monday. You can get breakfast here all day Tuesday through Saturday, but no grits after 11:00.

Less down-home in tone, the Restaurant at Cinnamon Hill is another place to eat in Lexington. See page 100 for particulars.

Lake Murray

LAKE MURRAY TOURISM AND RECREATION ASSOCIATION
P.O. Box 1783
Columbia, SC 29063
Located at 2184 North Lake Drive (Highway 6) near
Lake Murray Dam
(803) 781–5940

Lake Murray Tourism can provide maps showing all public and commercial marinas and landings, brochures, and a list of fishing guides.

A 50,000-acre man-made lake built in 1930, Lake Murray sprawls over seventy-eight square miles in the center of South Carolina. It is suitable for everything from canoes and sailboats to speedboats and party boats. It rates as one of the best fishing lakes in the country. A convenient swimming access is at one end of the dam, on SC 6, that crosses between Columbia and Lexington.

If you'd like to try fishing, the best way to get to know the lake and its possibilities is with one of the guides who work out of the twenty or so marinas and landings. The guides have

United States Coast Guard licenses known as six-pack licenses, meaning that they may take out up to six people at a time in their boats for fishing. These guides pass a rigorous exam about navigation, marine law, and weather; know CPR; and are tested for drugs. Your guide provides bait and tackle and takes you to the places where fish should be biting, then helps you do what it takes to catch them.

The guides specialize in striped bass, the most popular and plentiful fish in the lake. These are the fish people have mounted to hang over the fireplace. The largest striped bass on record caught in Lake Murray weighed forty-nine pounds.

You meet early in the morning, usually 6 or 7. The usual boat is the pontoon, equipped with live wells to hold bait and fish in a continuously changing supply of lake water, plus a sophisticated assortment of high-tech equipment such as a depth finder for finding fish. If the group includes females, a portable toilet probably sits in an inconspicuous spot somewhere; eight to ten hours makes a long day on the lake.

When you find the fish, your guide baits the hooks, casts the lines, and fastens the rods in place—more rods than people; each person usually watches two or three. When you get a strike, the guide will help you reel it in, get the striper off the hook, and tell you how to hold it up so that it looks extra big for a picture.

The cost of a guide is related to his or her celebrity and success at finding fish and to the number of people in the party. Figure in the neighborhood of $200 to $260 for two people for an eight-to ten-hour day, with gear and bait provided. You may pay more or less. Call ahead for rates and reservations.

If you want to fish for the largemouth bass, they're in there. Not many guides specialize in them, but you can try. A plastic worm is the most popular bait for largemouth bass.

Bream (pronounced "brim" and known as bluegills elsewhere) rate tops as a panfish, live in shallow water so you can even catch them from a bank or dock, and like real worms. For crappie (pronounced "croppie" in Virginia and known as spots further north) you just extend the rod and dangle the line, baited with a minnow. They're smaller, the record on the lake being about five pounds, and more suited to the pan than to the taxidermist, but they're fun to catch because, as one pro put it, "they fight like hell."

If fighting with fish seems unsportsmanlike to you, you can skip the fishing and simply boat. Boat rentals are available at Dreher Island State Park, Prosperity (803–364–3530). To get there, take Exit 91 off I–26. Go six miles southwest of Chapin off US 76. Signs point the way.

Also, Just Add Water, Inc. (803–345–9682), rents sixteen different kinds of boats, from Hobi Cats to party barges. They operate out of Putnam's Landing, Chapin (803–345–3040); Jake's Landing, Lexington (the site nearest Columbia, 803–359–9268); and Siesta Cove Marina, Gilbert (803–892–2978).

You need a South Carolina fishing license to fish on Lake Murray. For $11 you can pick up a nonresident license good for seven days at most sporting stores, stores near the water, and marinas. For detailed information phone the South Carolina Wildlife and Marine Resources Department (803–734–3888).

Aiken

Aiken is best known for Triple Crown horse racing in March, when the place is packed with thoroughbred horses and their people; but when that commotion is past, it's a great place to visit historic sites, look at beautiful old houses, walk the trails in Hitchcock Woods, and dine at the Willcox, where Winston Churchill and Franklin D. Roosevelt stayed.

It's easy to zip down to Aiken from Columbia by taking I-20 west toward Augusta. Exit onto SC 19 and follow it straight into Aiken. When you get into town, start by picking up a map for a self-guided tour of the area. You can do this at the Aiken Chamber of Commerce 400 Laurens Street N.W. (803–641–1111), which is open 8:30 A.M. to 5:00 P.M. Monday through Friday.

The tour mapped out by the Chamber of Commerce takes you past several Aiken landmarks.

Aiken County Historical Museum

    433 Newberry St. S.W.

    (803) 642–2015

    Open Tuesday through Friday 9:30 A.M. to 4:30 P.M. and the first Sunday of each month 2:00 P.M. to 5:00 P.M.

    Admission free.

The focal point is the building itself, a 14,000-square-foot house built in the 1930s by a Yankee industrialist. In addition to rooms furnished in the style of the 1900s, you'll find a display of agricultural equipment dating from the 1860s, old Aiken fire-fighting equipment, a medical and dental display, and a natural history room.

The best museum story is about a drugstore scene from the 1950s, when the Savannah River Project eliminated Dumbarton, the town where the store operated. The store was packed up and kept in a barn in a soybean field until 1980, when it was moved to the Aiken museum for display.

Hopeland Gardens and the Thoroughbred Racing Hall of Fame

    149 Dupree Place, one-half mile from SC 19

    (803) 642–7630

    The gardens are open 10:00 A.M. to sunset every day. The Hall of Fame is open Tuesday through Sunday 2:00 P.M. to 5:00 P.M.

    Admission free.

Nothing much blooms in the gardens in winter, but even then the place is worth a visit for its huge old live oaks, evergreens, fountains, and footpaths that are beautiful to walk any time of year. In spring and early summer it is a glorious palette of blooming color. The Hall of Fame, in a restored carriage house on the grounds, displays memorabilia, art, and photography.

WILLCOX INN
    100 Colleton Avenue
    (803) 649–1377
    Open for three meals a day Monday through Friday,
    breakfast and dinner on Saturday. Breakfast and dinner are
    served on Sunday, as well as buffet from noon to 2:00 P.M.
    All spirits available.

Eat or sleep in this impressive place and pick up a little history. In the old days, when you went to check in, the bellman stood behind you and looked carefully at your feet. The only people who were allowed in were those whose shoes the bellman approved with a nod. You had to be wearing Peels or Maxwells. People whose shoes were okay included Franklin Roosevelt, who always arrived at a special train stop below the inn. Today you'll be okay as long as you're wearing any shoes with clothing in the "nice casual" category.

The lobby has two huge stone fireplaces, rosewood pine woodwork from the area, and the original pegged oak floors.

The dining room attracts local folks celebrating special occasions as well as business travelers and tourists. It serves continental cuisine.

Camden

From Columbia you can drive to Camden, at the juncture of US 521 and US 1, close to I–20, in less than an hour. Another horse town, it is a thriving community of between 7,000 and 8,000 people, distinguished by being the oldest inland town in South Carolina. It is the home of steeplechase races, the Carolina Cup in April, and the Colonial Cup in November. Those knowledgeable about riding can tell you the area has a fine polo field and miles of bridle paths as well.

Of more interest to travelers without horses are the fine old houses, which you can see especially well if you walk around town, and Historic Camden, one mile south of downtown Camden.

George Washington slept here, too.

The site depicts life during the Revolutionary War period. The reconstructed Kershaw-Cornwallis House was the headquarters of General Lord Cornwallis during the British Occupation of 1780-81, and the site encompasses several other restored buildings as well, including two circa-1800 log houses. You'll also see small forts built by the British and the Powder Magazine, the only prewar military construction built by the colonists here.

A nature trail and picnic area are open to the public.

You'll learn a lot by browsing in the Historic Camden Exchange, a bookstore with an exemplary collection of Civil War material ranging from serious books to games and puzzles. For details about touring the buildings, phone (803) 432–9841 during normal business hours.

Newberry

You don't end up in Newberry by accident. You have to intend to go there. Although the community was settled in 1789 and I–26 nearly brushes the town's skirts now, nothing attracts your attention. You just don't expect to find anything beyond the fields and foliage when you turn off to follow the signs into Newberry.

When you get in the town, which has a population of about 10,000 people, most of whom seem to enjoy talking to just about anybody, you'll find whole blocks of historic buildings dating from the early 1800s, all listed on the National Register of Historic Places. Several of them are open to the public. Drive into the business district, which is also the historic district, to find them. Then park, walk on the sidewalks, and ask people questions. For maps, information, and printed material about Newberry history and architecture, go to the Newberry Chamber of Commerce at 1209 Caldwell Street (803–276–4274).

Sum Summer, a longtime resident of Newberry, suggests the following tour: "First, notice the old homes along Main Street. Many of the old oaks that once shaded the front yards of these homes were ripped up by tornados a few years ago, but there are still enough left so that you get a sense of how the town used to look.

"Stay on Main Street and you will pass the old Newberry Hotel on your right as you come to the old courthouse, which is now a community hall. The relief on the front of the building, an eagle with a palmetto tree in its clutches, symbolizes the hold the federal government had on South Carolina during Reconstruction.

"Pass the courthouse and turn right on McKibben Street for a view of the Newberry Opera House, built in 1888. The Barrymores once played here. Today the opera house is used as city hall offices. Turn back up Harrington Street and turn left on College Street to pass by Newberry College, founded in 1856. The campus has four buildings on the National Historic Register. One is a dormitory which once housed Confederate soldiers."

The library and courthouse in Newberry have information such as cemetery books and probate records available for browsing if you are interested in the genealogy of the early settlers. According to Ms. Summer, a surprising number of tourists find information about their families here.

From Main Street in Newberry, a drive of about five minutes on Nance Street to Mendenhall Road takes you to Carter and Holmes (803–276–0579), where you'll see some of the finest orchid greenhouses in the Southeast. The greenhouses are open weekdays 8 A.M. to 5 P.M., Saturdays to noon. Here the receptionist will lock your handbag or other items into a filing cabinet so that you can wander through the sixteen greenhouses unencumbered. You don't have to buy anything, but if you want to you can pick up cattleyas, phalaenopsis, cymbidiums, and other exotic plants as you go. When you're done, they'll total the bill and cheerfully put something back on the benches if you decide you're spending too much. Specially lighted displays in humidity-controlled cases show you how some of the orchids look when grown under perfect conditions.

Orangeburg

Orangeburg, an easy drive on I–26 from Columbia, is an old trade town settled in the 1730s and today still more a working, industrial town than a tourist place. However, the Edisto Memorial Gardens, on the North Edisto River (the longest blackwater river in the world), are famous among gardeners and worth a trip, especially if you are interested in roses. To get there, take Exit 145 from I–26 and go 7 miles. The gardens are open daily during daylight hours, and admission is free. You can phone ahead if you like: (803) 534–6211 or (803) 534–6821.

This used to be blackwater swamp land but has been transformed into a sort of blooming paradise with more than 300 rose varieties as well as the azaleas, dogwoods, and camellias which thrive over much of South Carolina.

The gardens memorialize a group of about 600 Confederate soldiers who tried to defend the Edisto River bridge and, in fact, did so until more Union troops came and hopelessly outnumbered them. What used to be rifle pits are now the gardens. They fill 110 acres and include a nature trail and a fountain dedicated to soldiers of World War I, World War II, Korea, and Vietnam.

The gardens' main event, the South Carolina Festival of Roses, is held the first weekend in May, when thousands of roses bloom. As many as 35,000 people attend the festival each year. In addition to garden displays, visitors can enjoy arts; crafts; live entertainment on two outdoor stages; and canoe, road, and bicycle races.

Sumter

Taking US 76/378 from Columbia, you can get to Sumter in an hour or less. The town is best known for Shaw Air Force Base, but the area has other interesting attractions and history that deserve attention too. The city got its name from Thomas Sumter, an important Revolutionary War figure. Another military note: the first shot of the Civil War was fired by a Sumter native and Citadel cadet at a Federal boat coming toward Sumter. But the area was spared much other fighting.

Sumter is a good place to shop for antiques; try the 200 block on Broad Street, where "antique row" offers a variety of shops in old houses. The shops are closed on Sunday.

Sumter is also a golf nut's haven, with more than twenty courses in the area. These courses offer package deals worked out with local motels. For detailed information, call or write the Sumter Conventions and Visitors Bureau at 21 North Main Street, P.O. Box 1149, Sumter, SC 29151 (800–688–4748 or 803–773–3371).

A good way to learn more about Sumter is to take one or all of the three driving tours mapped out by the Conventions and Visitors Bureau. This is one of the best community promotions projects in the country.

The Plantation Tour takes you from the Concord/Salem/Black River area, where the first settlers, who were herdsmen, came in 1735 to build cattlepens and cabins. The tour continues past Concord Presbyterian Church, built in 1841 on land donated by General Sumter, then goes on to sixteen more sites, including plantations, more churches, and the little town of Mayesville.

The Tour of Governors begins in the Rembert/Spring Hill area, where well-to-do planters went for summers in the early 19th century to avoid malaria at home. Another interesting stop on the tour is the Broom Factory and Craft Shop, where you can buy handcrafted gift items.

The Lakes Tour includes Battens Country Store and Restaurant and Wedgefield Presbyterian Church, an especially charming Gothic frame building from 1881.

Still other attractions in Sumter are listed below.

SUMTER COUNTY MUSEUM
122 N. Washington Street
(803) 775–0908
Open Tuesday through Saturday 10:00 A.M. to 5:00 P.M., Sunday 2:00 P.M. to 5:00 P.M.

The museum, housed in an Edwardian home, maintains exhibits, outbuildings, and formal gardens that give the visitor an idea of life in earlier times in the Sumter area. The house, built about 1845, was the home of Andrew Jackson Moses, his wife Octavia Harby Moses, and their fourteen children. It was subsequently inhabited by other families and finally donated to the Sumter County Historical Society in 1972 as a museum by the heirs of Tom and Martha Williams Bricer. The Bricers were the last people to live in it.

Artifacts from the Revolutionary war through Vietnam now fill a war memorial room. In another part of the house, the Textile Gallery displays vintage clothing from 1840 to 1940 and quilts from as early as 1820. Considering the number of children who lived in the house, the doll and toy collection seems especially appropriate.

An archives reading room is available for those interested in genealogical research.

Swan Lake Iris Gardens
West Liberty Street
(803) 773–9363
Open daily from 8:00 A.M. to dusk.
Admission free.

The gardens cover 150 acres and specialize in Japanese (or Kaempferi) iris. There are twenty-five varieties blooming from mid-May through June around the forty-five-acre lake and on its islands. Six different kinds of swans from all over the world swim on the water. Other flowers come into bloom all year long, so you can enjoy blooming plants even if you miss iris season. The place is set up for picnicking and playing, but you may not pick the flowers.

FLORENCE

Railroads have been an important part of Florence from its beginning in 1853. It has been a shipping center for tobacco and cotton, both widely grown in the area. During the Civil War, Confederate officials deployed soldiers from Florence. You drive through flat, mostly farming country to get here. Coming into town, you pass manufacturing enterprises of all sizes and realize that transporting manufactured goods and farm products still fuels the Florence economy. Trains are long enough and frequent enough to back up traffic on main arteries. In addition to being economically important in the area, Florence's farm products also provide an appealing tourist attraction.

Activities and Attractions

PEE DEE STATE FARMERS MARKET
Route 10, Box 15
Florence, 29501
On US 52 North, between Florence and Darlington
From I-95 take Exit 164, turn right, and drive one mile.
(803) 665–5154
Hours and days of operation vary seasonally, with weather, and with special events.

Farmers haul abundant supplies of fruits and vegetables in by the truckload to sell here, and the market sponsors special seasonal events to attract customers. For instance, on a Saturday in mid-April, for the Southern Plant and Flower Festival, vendors sell bedding and vegetable plants, house plants, and herbs in addition to whatever produce is available. On the last Saturday in June, the Pee Dee Summer Jamboree kicks off the beginning of the main produce season with arts and crafts shows and live entertainment. The first Saturday in December, the market focuses on Christmas trees and holiday items with Deck the Halls. Since the market is outdoors, weather is always a factor in what you'll find. Call ahead. When no one is in the office, a recording gives you current schedule and special event information.

FLORENCE AIR AND MISSILE MUSEUM
> Florence Municipal Airport Entrance, US 301 North
> From I-95 take Exit 170 and follow signs.
> (803) 665–5118
> Open every day usually 9:00 A.M. to 5:00 P.M. Hours may vary. Admission $5.00 for adults, $4.00 for senior citizens, $3.00 for children 4–16.

Signs outside the museum advertise "moon rock" and "Alan Shepherd space suit" to lure you in, but these are by no means the only things to see. Outdoor exhibits include about forty airplanes plus missiles and rockets from World War II. But to get back to the moon rock and space suit indoors, the rock is small and is reddish in color, in interesting contrast to the moon rock at the State Museum in Columbia that's been described as looking like a Milky Way candy bar. As for the space suit, it's white. At least it used to be. As the museum manager says, "It's been to the moon and it's a little soiled."

FLORENCE MUSEUM OF ART, SCIENCE, AND HISTORY
> 558 Spruce Street
> (803) 662–3351
> Open Tuesday through Saturday 10:00 A.M. to 5:00 P.M., Sunday 2:00 P.M. to 5:00 P.M.
> Admission free.

In addition to regularly changing exhibits of work by South Carolina artists, this museum offers some surprising collections that began because of the personal interests of people associated with it. For instance, because of the founder's interest in Southwestern Indian pottery, the museum acquired seventy-eight Southwestern Indian pieces with funds raised by a group of Florence women during World War I. Included is work by the important Hopi female potter Nampeyo, done about 1920.

A director in the 1950s who was interested in Oriental ceramics helped establish a collection of Chinese pottery and porcelain including a piece from nearly every dynasty. Visitors notice the pugnacious-looking figurines of Chinese boxers from the Tang Dynasty. There are also a few examples of Japanese work.

On a more local level, the History Hall features Florence County history, including a painting, *Francis Marion Crossing the Pee Dee*, done by Edward Arnold in 1857.

Lodging

Florence has a few dozen motels, ranging from Red Roof Inn (803–678–9000) to more expensive places such as the Holiday Inn at I-95 (803–665–4555) and the Quality Inn Downtown (803–662–6341). These are all of quality consistent with their counterparts elsewhere in the South. At this time there are no small inns, bed and breakfast inns, or European-style hotels.

Dining

BONNEAU'S
>   231 Irby Street
>   (803) 665–2409
>   Open for dinner Monday through Saturday from 6:00 P.M.
>   All spirits available.

You drive past Bonneau's when you drive through downtown Florence on US 52. The restaurant is in a restored 18th-century mansion and is decorated with antiques. Of the several dining rooms available, the glassed-in porch and the library, decorated to suit its name, are especially popular. Prime rib is on the menu every night. Other favorites are quail and chicken cordon bleu. Entrées come with salads and such specialties as stuffed potato Bonneau or rice or baked potato. If you explain special dietary needs to your server, the kitchen will accommodate you.

P.A.'s RESTAURANT
> 1534 South Irby Street (in South Park Shopping Center where
> SC 51 joins US 301 and 52)
> (803) 665–0846
> Open Monday through Friday for lunch and dinner, Saturday for dinner from 6:00 P.M.
> All spirits available.

In Florence this is the place many people recommend when you ask about a nice place to eat. The menu changes every day, featuring fish from the Carolina coast, aged beef, and fresh produce. Everything is made from scratch, including the desserts. "If you eat it here, it was made here," one person said. The restaurant's signature specialty is French Quarter fillet, a small fillet of beef topped with scallops, shrimp, scallions, hot peppers, and mushrooms.

The dining room is decorated in green and coral, with green and ivory tablecloths and napkins and lots of fresh flowers around the room.

Upstate

Clemson Horticultural Gardens
photo by Dan Smith

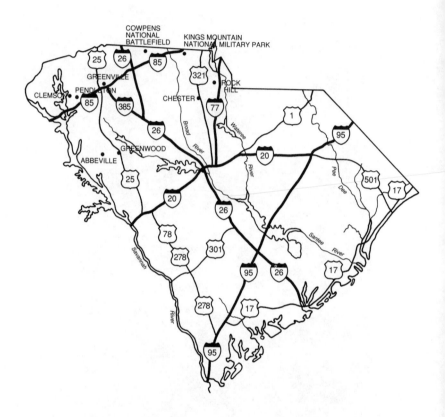

GREENVILLE

Like so much of America, Greenville originally belonged to
the Indians, in this case the Cherokees. In 1777 a treaty gave
the area to white men, and just shy of ten years later it had
become Greenville County. Before the Civil War, Greenville
was a mountain resort for wealthy Lowcountry planters, but
during Reconstruction it began to develop as a textile mill
town.

Greenville today is still a manufacturing community,
and the range of products has expanded to include plastics,
pharmaceuticals, and electronics. Partly because of the electronics industry, Greenville's citizens come from all over the
world, giving the city a surprisingly cosmopolitan atmosphere
for what is basically a Southern mountain town. Moreover,
the area is much prettier than most manufacturing towns,
with parks and gardens in the city, the Blue Ridge Mountains
rising above the downtown area, densely wooded suburbs,
and miles of rolling farmlands extending in all directions.
Greenville is home to Bob Jones and Furman Universities,
as well as two colleges, Greenville Technical and North Greenville.

Because Greenville and Spartanburg are such close neigh-
bors (not quite twenty-five miles apart by I–85 or US 26, and
sharing a common airport), attractions listed for Spartanburg
are also accessible from Greenville. Day trips from Greenville
and Spartanburg are listed together in the Spartanburg chapter (see page 136–142).

Activities and Attractions

GREENVILLE COUNTY MUSEUM OF ART
420 College Street
(803) 271–7570
Open Tuesday through Saturday 10:00 A.M. to 5:00 P.M.,
Sundays 1:00 P.M. to 5:00 P.M. Closed most major holidays.
Admission free.

The museum features a comprehensive permanent collection of Southern-related art in the United States from 1726 to the present. It shows the development of American art history using Southern-related examples. It also exhibits contemporary art, not limited to Southern work, of the 1970s and 1980s and has a growing collection of work by African American artists.

For years the museum was arguably Greenville's best-known attraction because it contained one of the largest Andrew Wyeth collections in the country. Word has been slow in getting around that the collection was sold; people still show up looking for it. The staff has worked hard to fill the gap left by its sale. They feel that what you find at the museum now is in some ways more interesting and better suited to the area. Among the museum's more familiar paintings you'll find one of the few portraits of John C. Calhoun painted from life. It was done in 1845 by John Healy. Another important regional work is William Ranney's *Marion Crossing the Pee Dee*, a first study for a larger painting on display in Fort Worth, Texas.

Other artists represented in the museum include Washington Alston, John Gadsby Chapman, Martin Johnson Heade, Jasper Johns, Georgia O'Keeffe, and Nancy Spero.

The gift shop sells work by local artists and crafters.

BOB JONES UNIVERSITY ART GALLERY AND MUSEUM
1700 Wade Hampton Boulevard
(803) 242–5100
Open Tuesday through Saturday 2:00 P.M. to 5:00 P.M.
Admission free. No children under six.

Bob Jones University is the largest nondenominational Christian liberal arts university in the world. This fundamentalist school is widely known for its collections of religious art, including work by Flemish, Dutch, German, French, Italian, and Spanish painters from the 13th through the 19th centuries. The Gallery of Sacred Art includes twenty-seven rooms with over 400 paintings, a collection of icons and vestments, and the Bible Lands Museum. Among the paintings you'll find works by Botticelli, Titian, and Rembrandt.

The rooms housing the paintings seem hushed and reverential, an atmosphere that Kevin Heisler, writing for the *Charlotte Observer*, called intimate.

In the icon and vestments collection, mannequins are dressed in garments of biblical times; in the Bible Lands Museum you'll find such features as artifacts from Pompeii and a Roman sarcophagus.

In keeping with the rules of the fundamentalist school, women may not enter wearing shorts or tight pants. Though this would seem unlikely in some cities, it's accepted here in this city of more than 400 churches.

GREENVILLE ZOO
150 Cleveland Park Drive
(803) 240–4310
Open daily 10 A.M. to 4:30 P.M. except Thanksgiving,
Christmas, and New Year's Day.
Admission $2.50 for adults, $1.25 for children 3–15.

Most of the animals in this fourteen-acre zoo live in natural, open-air exhibits. Displays include lions, miniature deer, kangaroos, giant tortoise, elephants, a waterfowl lagoon, and a collection of reptiles. Exhibits are interpreted in an education building.

ROPER MOUNTAIN SCIENCE CENTER
Off I–385 six miles east of downtown Greenville
(803) 281–1188
Observatory open every Friday night by reservation. Entire
Science Center open the second Saturday of each month
10:00 A.M. to 3:00 P.M. Planetarium open every Saturday;

show times 11:00 A.M., 12:30 P.M., and 2:00 P.M. Call for
information on the current show. Children under 5 not
admitted to the planetarium.
Admission $4.00 for adults, $2.00 for students and senior
citizens. General admission $2.00 for everyone for the
Saturdays when just the planetarium is open.

This facility, owned by the Greenville County School District, is billed as a learning center for children, but it is equally
fascinating for adults. The complex is at the top of a mountain
nearly 1,200 feet tall. It comprises a hall of science, a
hands-on discovery lab, a planetarium, and an observatory.
Outside on a living history farm, you can see how things used
to be done. Kids can wear off energy wandering through the
arboretum and walking the nature trails.

CAESARS HEAD STATE PARK
8155 Greer Highway
Cleveland, SC 29635
On US 276 northwest of Greenville at the state border
(803) 836–6115
Open daily year-round.
Admission free.

Some people believe the park got its name from a granite
outcropping that looks like a profile of Caesar's head; others
say it was named after a hunting dog named Caesar that fell
off the mountain in a chase. The park is 3,266 feet above sea
level. In addition to fabulous views, you can see a variety of
big birds, such as hawks and turkey vultures, flying into the
valley below. The entire site is rich in indigenous wildlife and
invites nature study, river fishing, and hiking.

JONES GAP STATE PARK
303 Jones Gap Road
Marietta, SC 29661
Off US Highway 276 3 miles northwest of Marietta.
(803) 836–3647
Open daily year-round.
Admission free.

Also a wilderness park, like nearby Caesars Head, Jones Gap is notable for its wide variety of plants, including many rare and endangered species. The splendid scenery includes the middle branch of the Saluda River flowing through a rocky gorge. Everything here is kept in its natural state, making it a good place to practice no-trace hiking.

Keowee-Toxaway State Park

> 108 Residence Drive
> Sunset, SC 29685
> 15 miles northwest of Pickens on SC 11 at Lake Keowee
> (803) 868–2605
> Park open daily year-round; interpretive center open
> Tuesday through Sunday 10:00 A.M. to 5:00 P.M.

Lake Keowee, a man-made lake of 18,500 acres, belongs to a project built by Duke Power Company, which has donated 1,000 acres to the state for use as a natural park. Known for the richness of its plant and wildlife, the park also has nature trails and some challenging hiking trails where no-trace hiking is expected. You can fish in the lake.

Twenty-four sites are available for tent and RV camping. All sites have water; RV sites also have electricity.

The interpretive center teaches about the Cherokee Indians, who for a period in the mid-1700s participated in trade with European settlers and, because of that influence, developed their own written language. *Keowee* means "land of Mulberry Groves," and *Toxaway* means "land of no tomahawks." These are translated today to mean "peaceful and serene." Though that wouldn't describe the final experience of the Cherokees, it certainly is true now.

Table Rock State Park

> Route 3
> Pickens, SC 29671
> On SC 11, 16 miles north of Pickens
> (803) 878–9813
> Open daily year-round.
> Modest parking fee charged in peak seasons.

Many native South Carolinians prefer Table Rock State Park as a vacation spot because it has all the wilderness charm and majestic views of the less developed parks in the upstate but still offers the creature comforts that make daily life easier, especially if you are traveling with children.

You need to make a reservation to be sure of getting into one of the 100 camp sites or fourteen cabins. From the restaurant you have a panoramic view of Table Rock Mountain.

As for activities, this park offers some of the most challenging hiking trails in the state, along with lake fishing and swimming. You can rent fishing boats, canoes, and paddle boats. Interpretive programs and the facilities of a nature center are available year-round.

Lodging

Just about every motel and hotel chain is represented in the general area, including the Hyatt (see below). These range in price from budget to high. There are also good places to stay nearby in Spartanburg (see pages 132–134) and farther away in Anderson, Pendleton, and Abbeville (see under day trips to these towns, on pages 136, 137, and 139, respectively).

HYATT REGENCY GREENVILLE
   220 North Main Street
   Greenville, SC 29601
   (803) 235–1234
   Rates: $59 to $110

The Greenville Hyatt has the glass-and-greenery elegance that typifies Hyatts everywhere. The great advantage of this hotel is its location in the city's downtown area, making it easy to walk the streets of the business district and see its restored buildings without having to get into your car. The hotel has two restaurants and a lounge, a swimming pool, and a whirlpool.

Dining

The Greenville area has restaurants ranging from the standard fast-food franchises to pricey continental dining rooms. Two of Greenville's best are listed below. You'll find more good restaurants in nearby Spartanburg (see pages 132–134) and farther away in Anderson, Pendleton, and Abbeville (see pages 136, 137, and 139, respectively).

DAMON'S
261 Congaree Road (Haywood Road at US 385)
Greenville
(803) 288–7427
Open daily for lunch and dinner.
All spirits available.

You'll probably eat too much if you go here, and it's a good thing you don't have to get dressed up to do it, because the specialties are racks of barbequed baby back pork ribs and onion ring loaves. The ribs are self-explanatory. The onion ring loaves are onion rings dipped in batter and then deep fried together so that they come out shaped like porous loaves. Other entrees include steaks, prime rib marinated in wine sauce and chargrilled, and barbequed chicken. Prices are moderate.

SEVEN OAKS RESTAURANT
104 Broadus Avenue
Greenville
(803) 232–1895
Open for lunch Monday through Friday, dinner Monday through Saturday. Closed Sunday.
All spirits available.

The restaurant is in a restored 19th-century mansion in the heart of old Greenville. It emphasizes historical atmosphere and gracious presentation. Specialties include beef, veal, and seafood.

Day Trips

See the section of day trips that begins on page 136.

SPARTANBURG

Spartanburg isn't the kind of a town you associate with picturesque attractions or tourist activities. Although it's in the foothills of the Blue Ridge Mountains, you wouldn't be tempted to say it "nestles" there. Travelers rarely say, "Oh let's go to Spartanburg" the way they would say, "Let's go to Charleston."

The early economic base was agricultural and to a large extent still is, although industry, especially textiles, has been important too. Much of the newer industry is international, creating a more cosmopolitan atmosphere than you'd ordinarily expect in a Southern Upcountry town. Perhaps because it is still relatively undiscovered, Spartanburg is one of the most interesting places in South Carolina to visit.

Along with its new culture, Spartanburg has history. The Cherokee Indians originally lived on the land, but they were pushed out of the way when the town was founded in 1831.

Spartanburg was named for a Revolutionary War militia called the Spartan Rifles, which won a battle at Cowpens that led eventually to the British surrender at Yorktown.

Greenville attractions, restaurants, and lodging facilities are also accessible from Spartanburg, as noted in the chapter on that city.

Activities and Attractions

WALNUT GROVE PLANTATION
  1200 Ott's Shoal Road
  Roebuck, SC 29376
  (803) 576-6546
  Open April 1 through October 31 11:00 A.M. to 5 P.M.
  Tuesday through Saturday, 2:00 P.M. to 5:00 P.M. Sunday;

127

November 1 through March 31, open only Sunday 2:00 P.M.
to 5:00 P.M. Closed Monday year-round.
Admission $3.50 for adults through age 50, $3.00 for adults
over 50, $1.50 for children 6–18.

Visiting Walnut Grove Plantation gives you an active sense of
what life in Spartanburg County was like in Revolutionary
times. In a guided tour of the main house, the detached kitchen,
and the school, you learn the plantation's history. Then you can
wander about looking into the other buildings at your leisure.

The plantation remained in the same family from the time
the land was granted to Charles Moore by King George III until it was donated to the Spartanburg County Historical Society in 1961 by Mr. and Mrs. Thomas Moore Craig. The
family kept detailed records, especially wills and inventory
lists. Because of that, the restoration, furnishing, accessories,
and recreations are uncommonly accurate.

The first formal education in the area began at Rocky
Spring Academy. The schoolmaster was the plantation owner
Charles Moore himself. He had taught in Ireland and apparently missed teaching. Just five years after establishing the
plantation, he gathered plantation and neighbor children to
start his school. Eventually he turned the teaching chores over
to a Presbyterian minister who did double duty.

But then this was a dual-purpose building. Two-seater
benches with attached desks and small slates attest to classroom activities; spinning wheels and looms reflect the other
work that was done here.

The doctor's office is a recreation of the one run by Dr. Andrew Barry Moore, the country's first physician. It originally
stood about a mile away, where you can still see the chimney. At
an audio station here a short tape recording gives you information from three of the doctor's journals. For as long as your nerve
holds out, you can peer at the old scarificators, bleeding bowls,
and other paraphernalia typical of early physicians' offices.

Outside, a nature trail about three-quarters of a mile long
takes you past the family cemetery and through a wooded
area; it ends behind the detached kitchen.

To get to the plantation take exit 28 from I–26 onto US 221. Turn left to go east, toward Columbia, on 221. At the first street past the intersection a sign will direct you the remaining mile to the plantation.

REGIONAL MUSEUM OF SPARTANBURG COUNTY
    501 Otis Boulevard
    Spartanburg, SC 29302
    (803) 596–3501
    Open all day Tuesday through Saturday except closed
    mid-day for lunch; open Sunday afternoon. Closed Monday.
    Admission free.

This two-room museum started, as such places often do, with a modest grant. Volunteers operate it with funds from civic organizations, mainly to provide exhibits related to local history. But, as one staff worker puts it, "the dolls took over."

And now the museum is like no other. The doll collection belonged to the grandmother of Helen Nott Sloan. Mrs. Sloan donated the collection to the local library in the early 1900s; in 1961 the library gave the collection to the museum. Today the collection of nearly 100 antique dolls has become one of the most popular exhibits in the museum and sometimes serves as the centerpiece for larger doll shows arranged by regional collectors and doll makers.

Other exhibits here include Indian artifacts, a few Revolutionary War weapons, Victorian furniture, and old maps.

Maybe the dolls really did take over, because a couple of life-sized mannequins are always dressed in old clothes, but their costumes change. One surprising day, visitors encountered a mannikin in a race driver's uniform at the entry to a museum feature on stock car racing.

PRICE HOUSE
    P.O. Box 786
    1200 Oak View Farms Road
    Woodruff, SC 29388
    To get to the Price House from Spartanburg take Exit 35 off
    I–26 and turn right onto Price House Road. You're there

when you come to a driveway marked with a sign leading to the house, surrounded by a chain link fence. Ring the cast iron bell at the entrance to get the guide's attention.
(803) 476–2483
Open April 1 to October 31 Tuesday through Saturday
11 A.M. to 5 P.M., 2:00 P.M. to 5:00 P.M. Sunday year-round.
By appointment all year. Closed Monday.
Admission $2.50 for adults, $1.50 for children 6–17.

Thomas Price loved to show off. He built this house on his 2,000-acre plantation in the late 1700s to be a showplace. Its architecture mixed steep Dutch gambrel roofs and inside end chimneys typical of Virginia and Maryland with walls one-board-wide like those prominent in Charleston. Price may have been a military deserter who learned about such a broad range of architecture because he covered a lot of countryside running away.

He certainly didn't hide once he established his plantation. He also ran the post office and a general store and had a license to provide bed and board for stagecoach travelers. The detailed records of all these activities have survived nearly intact, enabling the Spartanburg County Historic Preservation Commission to restore the property with unusual accuracy.

Restoration was a big job because transients living in the house at one time burned anything wooden they could find to keep warm. This included woodwork and doors. Only the shell of the house remained.

And although the bricks of the house were hand-made on the premises, Price apparently tried to cut construction costs by laying them with wet sand, with only a thin coat of mortar on the outside to hold everything together. The mortar chipped away, allowing the sand to dry and the bricks to fall, so restoration required rebuilding brick walls.

COWPENS NATIONAL BATTLEFIELD
Superintendent in charge: P.O. Box 308
Chesnee, SC 29323
11 miles northwest of I–85 and Gaffney and 2 miles southeast of US 21 and Chesnee. The entrance is northwest of the intersection of SC 11 and SC 110.

(803) 461–2828
Open daily year-round 9:00 A.M. to 5:00 P.M. except
Christmas.
Admission to the multi-image slide presentation $1 for adults;
$.50 for children 6–12. Admission to everything else free.

The Battle of Cowpens, fought on January 17, 1781, was
one of a series of victories in the South that led to the final
defeat of the British at Yorktown. What happened in the battle
is the stuff of Southern legends.

The battleground was a pasture called Hannah's Cowpens.
The British leader, Banastre Tarleton, led 1,100 practiced soldiers; General Daniel Morgan, a frontiersman and Indian
fighter, had 970 inexperienced men. Morgan devised an intri-
cate battle scheme designed to take advantage of the rolling
terrain and won the battle in just an hour. More than 800
British were killed, wounded, or captured. The Continentals
lost only a dozen men. Sixty were wounded.

Study Morgan's strategy at the exhibits in the visitors center, examine the memorabilia on display, and then follow the
walking trail across the battlefield where wayside exhibits tell
the full story.

HOLLYWILD ANIMAL PARK

P.O. Box 683
Inman, SC 29349
Take Exit 15 off I–26 and go 6 miles southwest on SC 292.
(803) 472–2038
Open daily 9:00 A.M. to 6:00 P.M. April 1 through Labor
Day, including holidays; 9:00 A.M. to 6:00 P.M. Saturday and
Sunday and weekdays by appointment Labor Day to
Halloween; Christmas drive-through Thanksgiving through
New Year's Day 6:00 P.M. to midnight.
Admission for regular tours $5.00 for adults; $3.00 for senior
citizens, handicapped, and children under 12. Admission for
the Christmas drive-through $1.00 per person.

These animals work in show biz. You've seen lots of them in
films, advertising photographs, and television commercials.

The park has one of the largest private collections of exotic animals in the Southeast and probably the largest collection of *famous* animals anywhere. Hand-raised and bottle-fed, they're comfortable around people. Like other celebrities, many of them can be fed and petted. The list of animals runs from African crown crane to zebra. In between are emus, ibex, pileated gibbons, pygmy goats, wallabies, and wildebeest.

Hollywild has a snack bar and gift shop as well as good picnic facilities. On weekends an "Outback Hayride" is available for a dollar extra.

CROFT STATE PARK
> 450 Croft State Park Road
> Spartanburg, SC 29302
> The park is off SC 56, 3 miles southwest of Spartanburg.
> (803) 583–2913 or 585–0419
> Admission free.

Croft used to be a World War II Army training camp. It's wooded and gently rolling, with fifty camp sites and a half-dozen picnic shelters. You can swim in the olympic-sized swimming pool and fish in the lake. Fishing boats and paddle boats can be rented at the lake. In addition to a nature trail, don't be surprised in this ex-Army training camp to find an exercise trail. Unlike some state parks, this one also has tennis courts and excellent bridle trails.

Lodging

Spartanburg has at least two dozen motels and hotels, most of them standard chains, along with a few strictly local places. You can also stay in nearby Greenville and farther away in Anderson, Pendleton, and Abbeville (see pages 136, 137, and 139 respectively).

COLLEGE MOTOR INN
> 491 E. Main Street
> Spartanburg, SC 29302
> (803) 582–5654
> Rates $24 to $40 including continental breakfast

This motel is in the heart of downtown, on a busy street near Converse College (a women's college). Its rooms are comfortable, with two extra-long double beds in each. And they're simple, with regular cable TV but no special extras. The rates are substantially less than those of the area's more elaborate hostelries. Continental breakfast, on the other hand, is "a little bit more," as one employee put it. Offerings include sausage biscuits, cereals, pastries, and a variety of muffins.

The motel is family-owned and has a reputation for treating guests like family. Check-in is simplified so that you don't have to do a lot of paperwork before you can go to your room. The motel has seventy units.

COMFORT INN WACCAMAW
      2070 New Cut Road
      Exit 17 off I–26
      (803) 576-2992
      Rates: $35 to $124 including continental breakfast

The special appeal of this motel is its location within walking distance of the Outlet Park, a large discount shopping center. In addition to standard rooms, some more elaborate quarters with king-size beds and Jacuzzis are available. Television includes HBO. There is a swimming pool. The Comfort Inn has 100 rooms.

COURTYARD BY MARRIOTT
      Hearon Circle
      Exit 72–C off I–85
      (803) 585–2400
      Rates: $39 to $82

One of the newer additions to the area, the Courtyard by Marriott is considered something special by many local people and employees. The place has lots of amenities: pool, Jacuzzi, three-meal-a-day restaurant, lounge, weight room, guest laundry, and HBO. "We emphasize friendliness," an employee said. "Even if you gotta grit your teeth to grin, you still gotta grin. We try to pay attention to the small things."

Meals in the restaurant feature poultry, fish, and pasta, with varied lunch specials. There are 108 rooms.

Dining

ANNIE OAKS
>   464 E. Main Street
>   Town Square Mall
>   (803) 583–8021
>   Open for lunch Monday through Friday 11:30 A.M. to
>   2:00 P.M.; for dinner Monday through Saturday 5:30 P.M.
>   to 10:00 P.M.
>   All spirits available.

This is a casual, pleasant, convenient place to eat when you are downtown. The entrées include fresh seafood, beef, poultry, and homemade desserts. Service is friendly and noticeably Southern, from the kind of folks who talk about "supper" rather than "dinner."

SPICE OF LIFE GOURMET MARKET AND RESTAURANT
>   100 Wood Row at John Street
>   (803) 585–3737
>   Open for lunch Monday through Saturday for dinner
>   Tuesday through Saturday.
>   All spirits available.

This restaurant is in a restored turn-of-the century foundry building. The interior walls are exposed brick; the lighting, which includes candlelight, is subdued enough not to feel like high noon on the prairie, yet bright enough to let you see what you're eating. Not that seeing is the most important element here; tasting is. Maria and Pat McCall concentrate on offering foods with exciting tastes and new flavor combinations. Their smoked trout pâté, for instance, is light and delicate with just a trace of smoky flavor and little nips of spice. One of their most popular entrées, "Designer Chicken," is baked chicken breast filled with a combination of goat cheese, toasted pine nuts, sun-dried tomatoes, and prosciutto. For less adventurous tastes, the menu includes more familiar dishes such as mixed seafood grill with tomato-basil sauce, grilled meats, various pastas, and veal. Lunch choices include vegetarian pasta, croissant sandwiches, and salads. Spice of Life has an excellent selection of wines.

In addition to the dining rooms, Spice of Life Market has a deli, kitchen shop, wine shop, bakery, and specialty foods section.

CAFE VIENNA
> 1200 E. Main Street, Suite 10
> (803) 591–1920
> Open for lunch and dinner Monday through Friday, only for dinner Saturday. Afternoon coffee and dessert served Monday through Friday.
> International Lounge serves all spirits.

Residents of Spartanburg interested in fine food consider this a serious restaurant. It serves classic continental food in a formal atmosphere complete with maroon table cloths and white linen napkins. Local art adorns the walls. Noretta Tocher, the manager, says her place has the best crabcakes in the Southeast. Crabcakes are among the changing daily specials on the menu. On the set menu, which includes Austrian and German entrées, the wiener schnitzel is probably the most popular. You have quite a few other choices too: pastas, breast of chicken or duck, rack of lamb, and pepper steak, for instance. On the extensive dessert menu, authentic Sacher torte, with German chocolate, apricot preserves, and almonds, is outstanding. You can order any of a dozen different kinds of coffee.

BEACON DRIVE IN
> 255 Reidville Road
> (803) 585–9387
> Open Monday through Saturday at 6:30 A.M. Closes at 11 P.M. first part of the week; hours extended to 11:30 P.M. Thursday, Friday, Saturday.

You can see signs on the major highways coming from the West Coast and from Florida telling you how many miles you have to drive to get to the Beacon Drive In. The place is famous—or infamous. Charles Kuralt once featured it on his "On the Road" television program.

The food is short-order: burgers, barbecue, sandwiches, fried chicken, french fries, onion rings, etc. The ambience— well, there isn't any. Menus listing more than a hundred items are posted on pillars where you can see them as you approach the cafeteria line. You're supposed to know what you want by the time you get there, and you're supposed to speak up immediately. If the clamor and hustle confuse you, the servers behind the counter may berate you for holding up the line. It's all part of the atmosphere. You can tone things down a bit by using curb service.

The portions are gargantuan. People usually make a second trip to the counter for huge desserts. Most famous are banana splits and ice cream sundaes.

Day Trips

Short drives from either Greenville or Spartanburg take you to interesting smaller communities with everything from historic sites to crafts centers.

Anderson

All sixteen blocks of the historic district of Anderson are on the National Register of Historic Places. If you decide to dine at 1109 South Main and Evergreen Inn, you might allow some extra time to walk the historic district. Also worth a visit is the Anderson County Arts Center at 405 North Main Street (803–224–8811). It's open weekdays 9:30 A.M. to 5:30 P.M., Sunday 1:00 P.M. to 3:00 P.M., and admission is free. Twelve exhibitions per year at the Art Center bring regional, national, and international art to Anderson. Several artists-in-residence programs and classes operate from the center.

You should also see the Anderson County Museum in the County Courthouse on Main Street (803–646–3782). It is open Wednesday, Thursday, Friday, and Sunday 2:00 P.M. to 4:00 P.M., and it is free too. There you'll see exhibits on local history containing artifacts and photographs.

A good place to eat in Anderson is 1109 South Main Restaurant (803–225–1109), open for dinner by reservation, closed Sunday and Monday (all spirits available). This is a Greek Revival-style mansion built in 1908. Because each of the small dining rooms is decorated in a different pattern and color scheme, they all seem like rooms in a private house. Peter Ryter, the Swiss chef and high-spirited owner, changes the menu frequently, always with interesting and tasty combinations. It could be smoked goose breast with raspberry sauce or a salad with hearts of palm and green peppercorns.

And if you'd like to spend the night, you can do that here too. The Ryters renovated the house next door to their restaurant and offer bed and breakfast accommodations in both buildings. The older one dates from 1834. One of its more spectacular rooms is octagonal and has built-in walnut and mahogany shelves. The walls are papered in a jungle-like pattern of peacocks and tropical plants. Rates are $60 to $75 a day, and the phone number is the same as that for the restaurant, (803) 225–1109. If you want to write ahead, address your letter to the Evergreen Inn, 1109 South Main, Anderson, SC 29624.

Pendleton

Pendleton is more than 200 years old and is remarkable because the entire town is on the National Register of Historic Places. Originally Cherokee territory, Pendleton was a center of business and political activity in Revolutionary times. Today it is a center for historic preservation and arts and crafts.

The Pendleton District Historical and Recreational Commission, in the old Hunter's Store across from the village green (803–646–3782), is a regional tour center where you can study historical exhibits and pick up cassette tape tours to the area. They can also arrange a tour of the Pendleton District Agricultural Museum, on US 76 next to the Woodburn Plantation. This museum displays farm machinery and tools from before 1925, including a cotton gin older than the one designed by Eli Whitney.

On the restored town square you'll find the Pendleton Farmer's Society Hall. It was originally intended as a courthouse in 1826, but after district changes eliminated its courthouse standing before it was finished, it became a farmers' hall instead.

Inside, the Farmer's Hall Restaurant and Tea Room serves lunch Tuesday through Saturday and candlelight dinners Friday and Saturday. The restaurant is famous for its desserts and sour cream drop biscuits. Phone (803) 646–7024.

Across from the Farmer's Hall, you can watch stoneware pottery being made at the Appalachian Crafters (803–646–8423).

If you think a day trip to Pendleton won't be quite enough, consider staying at the Liberty Hall Inn, 621 South Mechanic Street (about a half a mile from the town square on SC 28). You can phone at (803) 646–7500, and the zip code—if you'd rather write ahead than phone—is 29670. Rates are from $55 to $70. It's a comfortable place, furnished in period antiques; soft blues and roses are used in the drapes and linens. Every room has a good reading lamp on each side of the bed. All rooms have private bath and television, and no smoking is permitted in the rooms.

Throughout the house you'll find personal items from the family's own collection: pictures, needlework, books, quilts. Tom and Susan Jones and their son, Alex, have worked in the gardens to grow herbs, the biggest pumpkins in the county, and a flowering shrub border. When you're outside here you are really in the country.

The dining room is outstanding at Liberty Hall, and it's open for dinner year-round except Sundays and major holidays. Here the Joneses manage to make full use of all kinds of fresh local produce without ever cooking typical Southern dishes. Offerings range from delicate preparations of fresh trout to seafood entrées cooked just to the point of doneness. Many of the seasonings come from the Joneses' herb gardens.

All spirits are available, and the owners pride themselves on a good wine list with prices in an affordable range. The phone number for the restaurant is the same as that for the inn, (803) 646–7500.

Abbeville

In a quote that probably never gets said aloud, Abbeville is called "The Birthplace and the Deathbed of the Confederacy," because the first meeting of secessionists and the last cabinet meeting of Jefferson Davis were held here.

The most conspicuous buildings of the little town square are the Belmont Inn, which is on the National Register of Historic Places, and the Opera House, next door. In the early 1900s, the Spanish-style inn was a posh modern hotel where business travelers and performers appearing in the Opera House stayed, but as business changed and the theater became less important, the inn declined and eventually stood unused. Not until the mid-1980s was it restored and reopened, a project that, like the renovation of the Opera House, involved many in the Abbeville community.

You may want to spend more than a day in Abbeville, and with a dinner/theater/lodging package arranged by the Belmont in cooperation with the Opera House, you can have an experience as glamorous as that of Fanny Brice, Jimmy Durante, and Groucho Marx when they played in Abbeville. The Belmont's new splendor includes period reproduction furnishings in elegant rooms with high ceilings and paddle fans, but it still feels more like a country inn than a hotel. All rooms have private bath. Regular room rates are from $50 to $55. The inn's dining room, the Heritage Room, serves continental cuisine, with veal prepared a different way every day and various interesting dishes featuring chicken breasts. The desserts are excellent. The Heritage Room, popular with local folks as well as visitors who come to town to attend plays at the Opera House, is open for breakfast, lunch, and dinner, and spirits are available.

For dinner and/or room reservations, package rates and details, and a current theater schedule, call or write the Belmont Inn, 106 East Pickens Street, Abbeville, SC 29620; (803) 459–9625.

For more history, take a brief walk to the Abbeville Chamber of Commerce, 104 Pickens Street (803–459–4600), where you can pick up a map and a self-guiding tour of the community. Merchants on the square are apt to be standing in the doorways of their stores, if they're not busy, and will tell you all about Abbeville.

Greenwood

The main attraction for tourists in Greenwood is Park Seed Company, the largest and oldest family-owned mail-order seed company in America. The company, with its greenhouses, gardens, and gift shop, attracts visitors year-round.

The founder, George W. Park, printed his first catalog on a hand press in the late 1800s, when he was sixteen. He built his business in Pennsylvania but met and married a South Carolina county home demonstration agent specializing in horticulture. Eventually they set up the company in Greenwood, where the climate is temperate and the growing season long.

The entire Park complex is at this 500-acre location on Cokesbury Road (SC 254 North): seed and bulb storage and shipping, business offices, research, trial grounds and greenhouses, catalog production, even the photographic studio where all the pictures are taken for the catalogs.

The garden shop and greenhouse, which feature plants seeds, garden accessories, and upscale garden-related gift items, are open from 9:30 A.M. to 6:00 P.M. Monday through Saturday.

The outdoor trial gardens, where more than 70,000 plants are set and tended by hand, are open to the public any time during daylight hours.

The most popular time to visit is during the Greenwood Festival of Flowers in July, but you'll enjoy more personal attention in the less busy times. The gift shop greenhouses always have a wide assortment of indoor plants, including hard-to-find ferns and gesneriads. Spring displays are up and growing by February or March, depending on the weather.

If you take enough time looking around to warrant spending the night, you might try The Inn on the Square (803-223-4488) in downtown Greenwood. It was at different times a tire store, a warehouse, and a funeral home before being renovated and opened as a European-style forty-eight-room inn in 1986. These days practically everything social of any importance happens at the inn.

The rooms are furnished with antique reproductions. If you value quiet nights enough to ask for a room as quiet as the old funeral home, you can get one.

The inn dining room serves three meals a day and specializes in table-side cookery, including grilled seafoods and flaming desserts and coffees. New fettuccini concoctions have recently been added to the menu.

Some selections from the menu are served also in the bar-lounge, which is dominated by a large TV screen.

Clemson University

Known to football fans primarily as the home of the Clemson Tigers, the university, which is the center of the town of Clemson, deserves attention for some other features interesting to travelers whether they like football or not.

The best place to start is at the University Visitors Center in Tillman Hall, at the gateway to the campus. Here you'll find information about the university and the Upstate area and can pick up cassettes for self-guided tours of the campus. The center is open Monday through Friday from 8:00 A.M. to 5:30 P.M., Saturday from 10:00 A.M. to 4:00 P.M., and Sunday from 2:00 P.M. to 5:30 P.M. Phone (803) 656–4789. Tillman Hall is 11 miles from I–85 on US 76.

Gardeners will enjoy the University Botanical Garden, 250 acres encompassing the horticultural gardens, a forestry arboretum, and agricultural experiment stations. The gardens are noted for azaleas, camellias, a wildflower garden labeled in braille, and a rock garden with dwarf conifers. Choose among trails for hiking, jogging, and bird-watching.

Clemson has a significant number of historic buildings which you can see by following the Centennial Footpath, a walking tour with three different routes, which begins at Tillman Hall.

After the walk, you're entitled to an ice-cream cone from the Agricultural Sales Center in Newman Hall. You can also buy other dairy products, including Clemson blue cheese. Clemson dairy products are famous and delicious. Open Monday through Friday 9:00 A.M. to 5:30 P.M., Saturday 9:00 A.M. to 1:00 P.M., Sunday 2:00 P.M. to 5:30 P.M.

ROCK HILL

Rock Hill is a pleasant town of more than 40,000 people. Although the Scotch-Irish settled it in the 1730s, it didn't get its name until the mid-1800s when frustrated railroad workers came up with the name Rock Hill because of all the hard white rock they encountered digging. For a while it was just another little rural Southern town centered around a railroad depot; then it grew as a textile town. By the end of the century, Winthrop College had settled in, bringing emphasis on culture, the arts, and education.

Development of hydroelectric power plants on the Catawba River led people to call Rock Hill "an electric city."

Rock Hill is a quick drive down I–77 from Charlotte, North Carolina, and is home to many people who work in Charlotte. It is also a cultural resource for Charlotte residents. City managers like to say that Rock Hill offers the amenities of a much larger city but not the problems. To some extent that is true. In addition to Winthrop College and York Technical College, the city supports basketball, softball, professional baseball, art galleries, numerous historic sites, two city parks, the Rock Hill Little Theatre, and business and industrial parks. Rock Hill has its own distinctive personality and goals; it's not just a bedroom community to Charlotte.

To get a sense of the Rock Hill personality, take the David Lyle Boulevard exit off I–77. This is a limited-access stretch of highway, landscaped on both sides with enough care to make you aware of gradations in the height, texture, and shades of greenery.

The highway passes through a relatively new formal entrance to the city, called the Gateway. The Gateway comprises a circular landscaped plaza, two sixty-foot Egyptian revival pillars, and four thirteen-foot bronze statues. The city's first large-scale civic art project, designed by Michael Gallis, the Gateway is a gift from the city to its citizens to thank them for their effectiveness in developing long-range plans for the city. City officials call it "empowering the vision." It was accomplished by citizens' groups which met regularly to plan the city's future.

Every element of the Gateway means something in terms of their vision. The terra-cotta columns, which were saved from the demolition of the Masonic Temple in Charlotte, symbolize the historic significance of Rock Hill. The landscaped terrace suggests the city's gardens. Audrey Flack, from New York, was commissioned to create the four statues, which are identical except for the symbols they hold. One statue holds fire symbolizing the flame of knowledge, for the city's educational plans. Another holds a circle of stars, to represent the city's attention to culture. A third statue holds gears, symbolizing Rock Hill's business growth. Lightening bolts in the hands of the fourth statue stand for the city's functions and infrastructure and the role that the production of electricity has in its development.

Obviously you can't see all of this driving along the boulevard at speed limit. A parking area at the entrance allows you to pull over to study the project.

Impressive as it all is, you don't get the full spirit of the area unless you know also about the gateway at Leslie. Leslie is a development on the southeast side of the city where a pump house is protected by four poles from trucks and automobiles that might back into it. The man who owns it has painted the poles yellow, planted azaleas around them, and set up an eighteen-*inch* bronze statue. He says it's just to let Rock Hill know that Leslie has a gateway too. Some of the people who work in city management live in that area and pass the little gateway every night on the way home. They say they're flattered.

Activities and Attractions

WINTHROP COLLEGE
Oakland Avenue
Rock Hill
Office of College Relations (803) 323–2236

The college, now a little more than a century old, began as a teacher's college in a one-room building in Columbia, South Carolina, with just twenty-one female students. Its history and pleasing campus make it more interesting to tourists than colleges usually are.

The college moved to Rock Hill in 1895. The campus covers more than 400 acres. Students, enrolled in any of fifty areas of study, number about 5,000. The school became coeducational in 1974.

The campus, on Oakland Avenue, has been named a historic district. It has classical Neo-Georgian architecture, lots of grass, tree-canopied walks, a lake, and a fountain, all suggesting the archetypical notion of "college" that most of us have in fantasy. Two of the buildings, McBride Hall and Tillman Hall, are on the National Register of Historic Places. Also worth your attention, the Little Chapel, the building in which Winthrop's first classes were held, was moved from Columbia and reconstructed on the Rock Hill campus brick by brick in 1936. The building was built by Robert Mills, America's first architect, who designed the Washington Monument.

The Winthrop Art Galleries in the renovated Rutledge Building are open to visitors.

Lake Winthrop is also part of the campus, located about a mile away from the main buildings at the end of Sumter Avenue. Here visitors are invited to picnic, use the jogging track, and fish.

To pick up a campus map so that you can tour intelligently, stop at Tillman Hall, on Oakland Avenue in front of the water fountain.

MUSEUM OF YORK COUNTY
    4621 Mount Gallant Road
    Rock Hill
    Located off SC 161. From I–77 take exit 82A and head west. Museums signs mark the way.
    (803) 329–2121

The museum is open every day year-round except for major holidays.

Admission fees are nominal.

The museum generates a lot of local pride and attracts visitors, especially school children, from miles away. The Stans African Hall houses the most diverse collection of fully mounted African mammals exhibited anywhere in the world. Don't let the phrase "fully mounted" suggest heads with glass eyes and big horns lined up antler to antler on the walls. Animals are displayed in lifelike dioramas designed to show you something of their natural habitat and their relationship to one another. In one display, a large bird hovers near a tree, keeping clear of an elephant with tusks seemingly longer than its legs. The elephant towers close to viewers, giving youngsters a thrill and, sometimes, a case of nervous giggles because it all seems so real. The museum also has a hall displaying animals of the Western hemisphere, a planetarium, a nature trail with a rustic fenced overlook, and continuously changing exhibits in the art gallery.

A Hall of Electricity honors the area's important power production; a Hall of Yesteryear offers glimpses of how things used to be. Traditional local crafts and contemporary arts and crafts are exhibited too, and in a cheerful gift shop you can buy the work of local artisans.

A special gallery highlights the work of the illustrator Vernon Grant.

The museum is accessible to the handicapped.

There are picnic facilities on the grounds.

GLENCAIRN GARDEN
At Charlotte Avenue, Edgemont Street, and Crest Street juncture

Glencairn Garden is part of the inspiration for the landscaped terrace of the Gateway that honors Rock Hill's gardens. This city park covers six acres. In spring azaleas, dogwoods, wisteria, and tulips bloom either all at once or in rapid succession, depending on the weather. Paths wind through flowers and around a lily pond. A fountain centers the scene. Walking here is a peaceful respite from walking on the concrete sidewalks of the city and from riding in your automobile.

CHERRY PARK
Take exit 82B off I–77 and follow Cherry Road south about a mile and a half.

Cherry Park handles a variety of athletic events, including world-class softball tournaments. It's worth a few minutes of your time even if you don't care about the games to see the fourteen-foot bronze sculpture *Mighty Casey* by Mark Lundine. As an athlete, Lundine had a history of snatching defeat from the jaws of victory in the closing seconds of championship games. As a sculptor, he said he wanted to do a piece about losing in a clutch. *Mighty Casey* in defeat is the result, but his being in Rock Hill represents a victory because the citizens had to raise a substantial amount of money to lease the sculpture and even more to keep it.

Cherry Park covers sixty-eight acres and includes a one-and-a-half-mile lighted bicycle and jogging trail, picnic and playground areas, five softball diamonds, and five soccer fields.

Lodging

All the major motel chains are represented around Rock Hill at the I–77 interchanges. Local people have their favorites.

BEST WESTERN
1106 Anderson Road, 82B exit from I–77
(803) 329–1330
Rates: $35–$48

Often suggested by locals, the motel has rooms with facilities for the handicapped and nonsmoking rooms. The restaurant offers breakfast and lunch buffets. Cocktails are available in the lounge. The pool has a whirlpool. Entry to all rooms is from the inside.

ROCK HILL INN
   656 Anderson Road (US 21 bypass)
   (803) 329–2100
   Rates: $32 to $39

Located across from a business park, this used to be a Holiday Inn but has been refurbished since Holiday Inn moved to a new location. Traces of the past remain in such forms as a Holiday Inn identification stenciled on television sets that couldn't be blanked out completely by spray paint. The motel has 200 rooms, including accommodations for the handicapped and for nonsmokers. The restaurant serves breakfast and dinner. Cocktails are available in the lounge. This place is frequented more by repeat and long-term working people than by tourists. It may not be as slick as the newer motels, but it is more interesting.

Dining

In addition to its fast-food places, Rock Hill has two interesting and unusual restaurants.

TAM'S TAVERN
   1027 Oakland Ave.
   (803) 329–2226
   Open for lunch, cocktails, dinner every day but Sunday.

Situated in an old house of brick and cream frame, the restaurant is close to the campus of Winthrop College and reflects the college's interest in arts and letters. The interior is subdued, with dark green carpet on the floor, linen on the tables, and good art on the walls. The menu offers fairly standard contemporary favorites—crepes, salads, quiche, teriyaki chicken, and appetizers of fried cheese and veggies. Desserts are rich and gooey; they include almond Amaretto cheesecake and chocolate pastries.

HAMPTON HOUSE
>   204 Johnston Street
>   (803) 329–5958
>   Open for lunch Monday through Friday, also for dinner
>   Tuesday through Saturday.
>   All spirits available.

This structure, built in 1874, was Rock Hill's first big, fine home. It reflects the architectural revival that followed the Civil War. Located in the historic district, just off David Lyle Boulevard, it has been renovated to house a restaurant that attracts club women and business people for lunch and almost anyone wanting a special-occasion dinner.

A wide hall with a sweeping staircase serves as an entry and reception area. The downstairs rooms on either side of the hall are all dining rooms, each decorated according to a different theme. In one back room, for instance, dark green table linens and drapes patterned in foxes, horns, and hounds carry through a hunt theme.

The menu is contemporary upscale, with salads, grilled fish and meat specialties, and a sensational homemade black bean soup. Or choose from daily "country" specials, such as meat loaf or country ham with the appropriate vegetables. Yankees transplanted to Rock Hill sometimes order this, considering it Southern cooking. You don't have to listen hard to hear them discuss chitlins, okra, and other uniquely Southern food they haven't necessarily tried.

Meanwhile, often as not the local Southerners are eating marinated grilled chicken breast on a bed of crisp salad greens. A popular dessert is fresh fruit with a light boiled custard sauce.

Day Trips

From Rock Hill you can drive a short distance in any direction and find something interesting to see and do. With only a couple of exceptions you can avoid the interstates and get a good sense of what life in the South Carolina Piedmont is like.

Historic Brattonsville

On Brattonsville Road, Route 1, in McConnells (off SC 322 just north of the intersection with US 321), this restoration is open Tuesday, Thursday, and Sunday. You should call (803) 684–2327 for hours, since the schedule may change. Admission is $4.00 for adults from out of the county, $2.00 for adults who live in the county, and $1.00 for students 18 and under. For special events, admission for adults is half-price.

Historic Brattonsville is the kind of place that makes people who care about communities and their history smile because the impetus for its restoration has come from within the community itself. The York County Historical Society put a lot of money and energy into the restoration as a bicentennial project. They have continued to work on developing the place. The project is assisted by the South Carolina Department of Parks, Recreation and Tourism.

Historic Brattonsville is a restored village of 18th- and 19th-century structures erected by several generations of the Bratton family. Its restoration shows us the transition of an area from early settlements to large plantations.

Colonel William Bratton was an early settler and a wealthy officer of the local militia who led rebels to victory over British and Tory troops in a battle known as "Huck's Defeat" in 1780. The battle was important in mobilizing other Carolina frontiersmen against the British.

By the 1800s, the Brattons were even more wealthy. Their plantation was one of the most influential of the time, and they had a hand in everything going on in the area. Because it was about midway on the main road from Lincolnton and Gastonia to Columbia, the plantation was an important stop for changing horses.

Reliable documentation such as store and church records ensured gratifying accuracy in Brattonsville's slow restoration. The guided tour includes a replica of a 1750s dirt-floored backwoodsman's cabin, the Scotch-Irish McConnell family's cabin, the female academy, an authentic antebellum home, and a number of other sheds and buildings. The restored homes are furnished in period furniture including Bratton family pieces displayed along with such old-time utilities as a biscuit press and a tin bathtub.

As restoration progresses, you'll be able to go back year after year and find something new each time.

Historic Brattonsville differs from many restoration projects in that if it's closed when you stop, you are still invited to walk around the grounds and peer into the windows. Rich Ellison, a staff member, says, "All we ask is that you be sure to close the gates when you leave so that the animals don't get out." It seems that not long ago the mule got out and did in a neighbor's garden.

Kings Mountain National Military Park and Kings Mountain State Park

Kings Mountain National Military Park, on Park Road off SC 216 (803–936–7931), and Kings Mountain State Park, next door at 1277 Park Road (803–222–3209), may be confused because of their nearly identical names. The first is open daylight hours year-round and has free admission. The state park is open every day from 7:00 A.M. to 9:00 P.M. Admission is free, but there is a parking fee in the busier months: $2.00 for cars and motorcycles, $7.00 for multipassenger vehicles.

Both parks are named for Kings Mountain, a sixteen-mile-long range. The national park commemorates the Battle of Kings Mountain on October 7, 1780, in which the mountain men beat the Tory forces after marching 179 miles in eleven days to get there. You can tour the Revolutionary War battleground for a nip of history and get the full story from the interpretive center there. A large stone marks the grave of Col. Patrick Ferguson, the professional Tory soldier who was killed leading his forces against the mountain soldiers.

At Kings Mountain State Park, a living farm museum recreates a typical frontier homestead of the South Carolina Upcountry in 1840. You'll get a glimpse of the kind of life that created mountaineers tough enough to march for eleven days and then whip Tories. On a less bellicose note, Kings Mountain has more than 100 campsites. You can explore the hiking trails and lunch in a shady picnic shelter. You can swim and fish in the lake and rent canoes, fishing boats, and pedal boats.

Chester

In a sense, two of Chester's attractions are related: the Cruse Vineyards and Winery and the Skydive Carolina Parachute Center. The idea is that most folks would have to be a little drunk before they'd even think about skydiving. However, the connection is more imagined than real. You wouldn't be welcome to skydive if you were skunked. And the first steps are safe and conservative—instruction and indoor classroom training with a static line. Classes are offered weekends. You register at the Chester airport, on SC 909 west of US 321. Phone (803) 581–JUMP.

The Cruse Vineyards and Winery, on Woods Road off SC 72, offers tours and tastings of red, white, and blush wines. The tasting room is open Friday and Saturday afternoons, though you may be able to make an appointment for another time. Phone (803) 377–3944.

A more conventional attraction is Chester State Park, which has campsites, picnic shelters, lake fishing, and fishing boat rentals. Smaller than many of South Carolina's state parks, with hills looking onto a sixty-five-acre lake, this is considered by many to be one of the nicest, most peaceful parks in the state. It is on SC 72, 3 miles southwest of Chester. The park is open daylight hours every day. Admission is free. Phone (803) 385–2680.

Carowinds

P.O. Box 410289
Charlotte, NC 28241
On I–77 10 miles south of Charlotte, 12 miles north of Rock Hill

(800) 822–4428, (704) 588–2600, or (803) 548–5330
Hours and days when Carowinds is open vary seasonally, as
does admission. Call or write for schedules and admission
fees on specific dates.

Although Carowinds is barely over the North Carolina border into South Carolina, about 10 miles south of Charlotte, it
is considered an attraction for Rock Hill, from which it is a
dozen miles north on I–77. More or less sitting on the state
border, Carowinds is the most popular theme park in the two
states. It covers eighty-three acres and attracts well over a million people a year with its rides, concessions, campground,
theaters, wave pool, and water slides.

Even standing in the field outside the fence, you can hear
the shrieks, presumably of pleasure, from people riding Thun-
der Road, the giant roller coaster that takes you up to speeds
of sixty miles per hour, and the Rip Roarin' Rapids, a man-
made whitewater rapids ride. All the loops and falls and
whirls make Carowinds seem a good place for a Dramamine
concession.

For those inclined to keep their feet firmly on the ground,
some of the theme areas encourage more stable activities. For
instance, the main entrance of the park features Plantation
Square, a shopping area modeled on the Charleston waterfront. And Blue Ridge Junction has log cabins and crafts re-
flecting the Appalachian Mountains. Carowinds has a
campground (704–588–2606), and there is a nice Comfort
Inn across the road (803–329–2171). Rates for the campground are moderate.

STATE PARKS

Central State Park Office: South Carolina State Parks
1205 Pendleton Street, Columbia, SC 29201
(803) 734–0156

Upstate

CAESARS HEAD
8155 Geer Highway
Cleveland, SC 29635
(803) 836–6115

CROFT
450 Croft State Park Road
Spartanburg, SC 29302
(803) 585–1283

DEVILS FORK
161 Holcombe Circle
Salem, SC 29676
(803) 944–2639

JONES GAP
303 Jones Gap Road
Marietta, SC 29661
(803) 836–3647

KEOWEE-TOXAWAY
108 Residence Drive
Sunset, SC 29685
(803) 868–2605

KINGS MOUNTAIN
1277 Park Road
Blacksburg, SC 29702
(803) 222–3209

LAKE HARTWELL
19138–A South SC 11
Fair Play, SC 29643
(803) 972–3352

OCONEE
624 State Park Road
Mountain Rest, SC 29664
(803) 638–5353

PARIS MOUNTAIN
2401 State Park Road
Greenville, SC 29609
(803) 244–5565

SADLERS CREEK
940 Sadlers Creek Park Road
Anderson, SC 29624
(803) 226–8950

ROSE HILL PLANTATION
Sardis Road, Route 2
Union, SC 29379
(803) 427–5966

TABLE ROCK
246 Table Rock State Park
Road
Pickens, SC 29671
(803) 878–9813

Upper Midlands

ANDREW JACKSON
196 Andrew Jackson Park
Road
Lancaster, SC 29720
(803) 285–3344

DREHER ISLAND
Route 1, Box 351
Prosperity, SC 29127
(803) 364–3530

HAMILTON BRANCH
Route 1, Box 97
Plum Branch, SC 29845
(803) 333–2223

BAKER CREEK
Route 1, Box 219
McCormick, SC 29835
(803) 443–2457

CALHOUN FALLS
Route 1, Box 360–A
Calhoun Falls, SC 29628
(803) 447–8267

HICKORY KNOB
Route 1, Box 199–B
McCormick, SC 29835
(803) 391–2450

CHESTER
Route 2, Box 348
Chester, SC 29706
(803) 385–2680

LAKE GREENWOOD
302 State Park Road
Ninety Six, SC 29666
(803) 543–3535

LAKE WATEREE
Route 4, Box 282 E–5
Winnsboro, SC 29180
(803) 482–6126

LAKE RUSSELL ACCESS
Route 3, Box 435
Iva, SC 29655
(803) 348–7841

LANDSFORD CANAL
Route 1, Box 423
Catawba, SC 29704
(803) 789–5800

SESQUICENTENNIAL
9564–D Two Notch Road
Columbia, SC 29223
(803) 788–2706

Lower Midlands

AIKEN
1145 State Park Road
Windsor, SC 29856
(803) 649–2857

LEE
Route 2, Box 202
Bishopville, SC 29010
(803) 428–3833

BARNWELL
Route 2, Box 147
Blackville, SC 29817
(803) 284–2212

LYNCHES RIVER
Route 1, Box 223
Coward, SC 29530
(803) 389–2785

CHERAW
Route 2, Box 888
Cheraw, SC 29520
(803) 537–2215

POINSETT
6660 Poinsett Park Road
Wedgefield, SC 29168
(803) 494–8177

GOODALE
650 Park Road
Camden, SC 29020
(803) 432–2772

REDCLIFFE PLANTATION
181 Redcliffe Road
Beech Island, SC 29841
(803) 827–1473

RIVERS BRIDGE
Route 1
Ehrhardt, SC 29081
(803) 267–3675

WOODS BAY
Route 1, Box 208
Olanta, SC 29114
(803) 659–4445

SANTEE
Route 1, Box 79
Santee, SC 29142
(803) 854–2408

Lowcountry and Coastal

CHARLES TOWNE LANDING
1500 Old Towne Road
Charleston, SC 29407
(803) 556–4450

HAMPTON PLANTATION
1950 Rutledge Road
McClellanville, SC 29458
(803) 546–9361

COLLETON
Canadys, SC 29433
(803) 538–8206

HUNTING ISLAND
1775 Sea Island Parkway
St. Helena Island, SC 29920
(803) 838–2011

EDISTO BEACH
8377 State Cabin Road
Edisto Island, SC 29438
(803) 869–2156

HUNTINGTON BEACH
Murrells Inlet, SC 29576
(803) 237–4440

GIVHANS FERRY
746 Givhans Ferry Road
Ridgeville, SC 29472
(803) 873–0692

LAKE WARREN
Route 1–A, Box 208–D
Hampton, SC 29924
(803) 943–5051

LITTLE PEE DEE
Route 2, Box 250
Dillon, SC 29536
(803) 774–8872

OLD DORCHESTER
300 State Park Road
Summerville, SC 29485
(803) 873–1740

MYRTLE BEACH
US 17 South
Myrtle Beach, SC 29577
(803) 238–5325

OLD SANTEE CANAL
900 Stony Landing Road
Moncks Corner, SC 29461
(803) 899–5200